The Penn State Series in German Literature

Wilhelm Müller, The Poet of the Schubert Song Cycles: His Life and Works, by
Cecilia C. Baumann

German Baroque Poetry, 1618–1723, by Robert M. Browning

German Poetry in the Age of the Enlightenment, by Robert M. Browning

Richard Beer-Hofmann: His Life and Work, by Esther N. Elstun

Kafka's Narrative Theater, by James Rolleston

War, Weimar, and Literature: The Story of the Neue Merkur, 1914–1925, by Guy
Stern

The Leitword in Minnesang: A New Approach to Stylistic Analysis and Textual
Criticism, by Vickie L. Ziegler

Georg Trakl's Poetry

Max von Esterle:

Widmung für Georg Trakl

Georg Trakl's Poetry
Toward a Union of Opposites

Richard Detsch

The Pennsylvania State University Press
University Park and London

Published with the cooperation of the Austrian Institute.

Library of Congress Cataloging in Publication Data

Detsch, Richard.
Georg Trakl's poetry.

Includes bibliography and index.
1. Trakl, Georg, 1887–1914—Criticism
and interpretation.   I. Title.
PT2642.R22Z593   1983   831′.912   82-42780
ISBN 0-271-00343-X

Designed by Dolly Carr

Printed in the United States of America

Contents

Acknowledgments

Without the generous financial help of the Austrian Institute and the Research Services Council of Kearney State College the publication of this book would not have been possible. My sincere thanks go, in particular, to Dr. Fritz Cocron, the director of the Austrian Institute, and to Dr. Thomas Flickema, the dean of the Graduate School at Kearney State College, for their personal efforts in support of publication.

I also owe a debt of gratitude to Dr. Walter Methlagl, the director of the *Brenner* Archives at the University of Innsbruck. His encouragement over the years contributed in no small measure to my determination to bring this work to its conclusion. He has, in addition, a claim to my acknowledgment for his permission to use the archival resources and to reprint the illustration by Max von Esterle dedicated to Georg Trakl which appeared in the *Brenner* issue of July 15, 1913.

Introduction:
In Search of a New Reality

Georg Trakl was born in Salzburg on February 3, 1887, and died of cocaine poisoning in a military hospital in Krakow on November 3, 1914, while under observation for his mental condition. He had been serving on the Russian front as a medic in the Austrian army. A pharmacist by occupation, he had been unsuccessful in attaining even a small measure of professional stability prior to the outbreak of the war. As for his literary ability, it wasn't until after his May 1912 meeting in Innsbruck with Ludwig von Ficker, the publisher of the *Brenner,* the then-avant-garde periodical of literature and cultural criticism in which much of Trakl's mature poetry was to first appear, that Trakl began to gain the recognition he deserved. By the poet's own admission, he was given to periods of intense melancholy and, by a more disguised confession in his poetry, to feelings of intense guilt resulting, apparently, from an incestuous relationship with his sister. He tried to overcome his depression by heavy use of the alcohol and drugs which eventually caused his death.

Trakl ranks with Georg Heym, who also died young—at twenty-five—and Gottfried Benn, and above Ernst Stadler, as one of the great poets of the early, most creative period of German Expressionism. His significance in this century is, of course, exceeded by that of another Austrian poet, Rilke, who lived longer and produced poetic creations in greater volume. Rilke's is largely a cerebral poetry, richer in its more clearly defined periods of development and in its articulation of a Weltanschauung; Trakl's is the lyric voice of despair and hope in an often indistinguishable, chaotic mixture—a deeply personal revelation that reflects as well the unarticulated experiences and fantasies of his contemporaries. In spite of these fundamental differences Rilke would, shortly after Trakl's death in letters to Ludwig von Ficker, pay homage to Trakl's unique poetic gifts.[1]

The same indications of intensely felt despair and hope, as well as the strong undercurrent of guilt, sharply distinguish Trakl's poetry from that of French Symbolism, particularly from that of Rimbaud, to which Trakl clearly owes much of his poetic style and imagery. The exotic, tantalizing collage of images without basis in reality is a standard feature in the work of both poets; but Trakl's employment of this technique cannot be explained solely by reference to his French predecessor.

Today, anyone undertaking an interpretation of Georg Trakl's poetry must come to terms with the decisive turn which Trakl criticism took in the late 1950s when a dispute arose between the proponents of two diametrically opposed critical approaches. The lines of this dispute were drawn by Eduard Lachmann and Walther Killy in their conflicting analyses of Trakl's poem "Passion."[2] Lachmann stressed the Christian elements of the poem, especially the hope of redemption which it expressed, and attempted to interpret the entire poem from the Christian perspective, as he had done with all of Trakl's poetry. Taking issue with this type of interpretation, Killy emphasized instead the so-called Orphic aspects of "Passion"—the attempt of the artist to gain a purely aesthetic mastery over a world in hopeless disarray, a world without redemption.

Since that time, following Killy's interpretation, critics have generally abandoned the search for a possible area of coherent significance behind the often illogical flow of images and have concentrated instead on matters of lyrical style and structure.[3] The opacity of this poetry itself, perfectly in accord with much of modern poetry, as well as the lack of theoretical statements by the poet and the dearth of commentary in his scanty correspondence have certainly been important factors in this new orientation. Indeed it seems surprising that earlier critics could have established dominant metaphysical and exegetical trends with their analyses. No doubt the influence of Trakl's friend and patron Ludwig von Ficker was crucial in determining the direction of such criticism, for his periodical took a marked turn toward Roman Catholic religiosity after Trakl's death.[4]

In my own work, I have attempted to steer clear of the pitfalls of arbitrary text manipulation into which Lachmann, in his exegetical approach, has frequently stumbled. At the same time I maintain that Trakl's poetry itself provides the enticement for the reader to ponder its meaning. Indeed, Killy's own injunction against attempting to find "Bedeutung" or "Sinn" in Trakl's poetry[5] does not prevent him from fixing the significance of the *Brenner* version of Trakl's "Passion" in "das zauberische Spiel des Orpheus"[6]—a poem which, as Killy earlier claims, lives "im Übergang einer Perspektive in die andere: nie ist Orpheus ganz Orpheus, er zielt darauf, auch Christus zu sein, oder der Dichter."[7] In concluding with an emphasis of the Orpheus perspective at the expense of the other two, Killy is at odds with his own interpretation.

I recognize that any thread of meaning in Trakl's poetry cannot lead too far, but I do not therefore refuse to follow such a thread. I tend to agree with Killy's finding that in Trakl's poetry many recurring persons, things, and attributes (e.g., "der Fremdling," "der Ungeborene," "der Knabe," "Brot und Wein," "Haus," "Tier," "Vogelflug," "blau," "weiss," "schwarz," "dunkel") are impenetrable "Chiffren"[8] with no coherent frame of reference, no determinable thing symbolized behind them. On the other hand, I am convinced that some of these images do indicate certain feelings of the poet which cannot be dismissed merely by a reference to the words in one of his letters: "Es ist ein so namenloses Unglück, wenn einem die Welt entzweibricht."[9]

The following interpretation is based upon the premise that the lines of the critical dispute were falsely drawn. The issue is not whether this poetry gives evidence of the poet's religious inclinations or whether it is a purely aesthetic endeavor. Several critics, notably Klaus Simon in his *Traum and Orpheus*, have acknowledged that both aspects are represented in Trakl's poetry. The question should be rather whether this poetry, both in style and content, gives evidence only of a world in hopeless disarray, or whether, even within this chaotic world, there are signs of the dawning of a different reality—a reality which is neither strictly Christian nor merely an aesthetic creation.

Here I attempt to show that Trakl's poetry does indeed contain indications of the poet's perception of a different reality, the nature of which is unity. The world usually perceived under the aspects of concreteness and individuation appears in hopeless disintegration in Trakl's poetry. But from it the new world of oneness emerges, the union of subject and object, of the poet and that which surrounds him. The awareness of this kind of unity is as ancient as the great religions of the East, but it seems to be growing at an accelerated rate in our own century, especially through the advances in the natural sciences and certain new insights in the fields of psychology and philosophy. Indeed, it would seem that the dominant experience of our time is that of a world rapidly converging to form "one" world in every respect. I have devoted the last chapter of this work to a more specific determination of the concept of unity in the light of the opinions of such modern exponents as Erich Neumann, Gottfried Benn, C. G. Jung, Erich Fromm, Pierre Teilhard de Chardin, and Romano Guardini.

In the course of their interpretations, several Trakl critics have alluded to something resembling the concept of unity. None of them, however, has yet made this concept the focal point of an entire investigation.[10] Probably the most extensive treatment given to this aspect of Trakl's poetry is that of Heinrich Goldmann in his *Katabasis,* especially in the chapter entitled "Die Schwester." Goldmann interprets Trakl's incest motif from a Jungian standpoint as indicative of a subconscious desire for an integration of the personality, a union of "animus" with "anima."[11] Part I of my own interpretation, where the topics of incest and androgyny are pursued, is largely in accord with the work of Goldmann. Here I interpret the *Brenner* version of "Passion" and the prose poems "Traum und Umnachtung" and "Offenbarung und Untergang" with special emphasis on the recurring incest motif. In order to counter Killy's claim that there is no logical context in "Passion" and to prepare the way for other poem analyses, I devote much space, in particular, to the analysis of "Passion."

Part I documents the way in which Trakl's search for unity leads to the fusion of brother and sister into one sex. Part II deals with the union in death of all Trakl's human figures and the different periods of life they represent. On the basis of an interpretation of Trakl's poem "Allerseelen," I try to establish, first of all, that Trakl's attitude toward death is related, in some of its characteristics, to the Romantic and Neoromantic traditions. Then I turn to the analysis of the *Brenner* version of "Abendland" in order to show that stillbirth is as central to this poem as incest is to "Passion."

In an effort to understand the theme of death and the function of time in Trakl's poetry, I draw upon Martin Heidegger's interpretation of Trakl's work.[12] Most critics reject Heidegger's contribution as a philosopher's unwarranted encroachment on literary criticism; some few approve but without really coming to grips with the philosophy of *Sein und Zeit* upon which Heidegger's interpretation is predicated.[13] Since I am largely in agreement with the essential

ideas of Heidegger's much maligned and misunderstood interpreta-
tion, I felt it necessary to pursue these ideas to their source in order
to lend them additional clarity and credence.

Parts I and II deal respectively with what can be considered the
major thematic patterns of Trakl's poetry, incest and death, both of
which are ultimately signs of wholeness or the union of opposites.
The first two chapters of Part III examine other aspects of Trakl's
poetry which indicate unity but which are not exclusively related to
incest and death. Chapter 6 discusses the union of good and evil
which is basic to all of Trakl's poetry and devotes special attention to
his uncompleted puppet play, *Blaubart*, as well as to the prose
poem "Verwandlung des Bösen." Chapter 7 takes up the analysis of
elements of style in Trakl's poetry. Here I employ the term "sym-
bolic" in Goethe's sense to indicate that Trakl's poetic language itself
points to a higher reality—to unity. The goal for both poets is identi-
cal; the means, however, are different. Through the avoidance of
concreteness and individuation in his poetry, Trakl opens the way to
the experience of unity. Goethe sees in the concrete object a mani-
festation of the unity ("das ewig Eine") which is its actual essence.
The final chapter, besides attempting to define more precisely the
meaning of unity and to justify its applicability in an analysis of
Trakl's poetry, turns once again to Killy's Trakl interpretation and
explains in more detail the fundamental divergence between Killy's
conclusions and mine.

All quotations of Trakl's works and letters are from the critical
edition, edited by Walther Killy and Hans Szklenar and published in
1969. In the course of the analyses of particular works, I make fre-
quent reference to variant wordings as contained in the second
volume of this two-volume edition.

A comment about the more general methodology of this interpreta-
tion is also in order. I felt that a division into parts would help focus
attention more clearly on the relationship of the elements discussed
in the various chapters. In order to further emphasize the function of
each of the parts as a unit, I have numbered the notes in each part
sequentially. The reader will notice, however, a difference between
the treatment of materials in the first two parts and in the third part.
The former are built around the analyses of single poems, but since
no analysis of any one Trakl poem is complete without abundant
reference to many of his other poems and works, several of the im-
portant points touched upon in the course of the discussion of "Pas-
sion" (e.g., the death theme) receive further elucidation in the
discussion of other poems in subsequent chapters. Also, some of the

conclusions reached from the analysis of one poem are, with a certain amount of qualification and reformulation, found to be applicable to other poems. For these reasons and also because the themes of incest and death are intimately related in Trakl's works, the chapters of Parts I and II are more closely interrelated than those of Part III. The latter serves to draw together some additional considerations which are of major importance but which could not be presented earlier without interrupting the development of the two preceding parts.

   None of the conclusions reached in the individual chapters should be considered as complete in themselves. All are intended to relate to the ultimate union of opposites, the hymeneal joining of the poet and the world. And yet the unity which is reflected in Trakl's poetry is never precisely defined by him nor is it ever concretely realized. The incest motif, the dead child motif, the conjunction of good and evil, the absence of concreteness and individuation—these are all merely indications which must be considered *in toto* if a more convincing impression is to be gained. The unity in Trakl's poetry is revealed basically only through an indistinct yearning—a search, as the poet writes in the earlier version of "Passion": "Ein Leichnam suchest du unter grünenden Bäumen / Deine Braut . . ." (I: 393).

Part I:
Incest and Androgyny

Aber strahlend heben die silbernen Lider die Liebenden:
Ein Geschlecht. Weihrauch strömt von rosigen Kissen
Und der süsse Gesang der Auferstandenen.
(from "Abendländisches Lied")

1
Incest in Trakl's Works

In his application of the term "Chiffre," Killy seems to be referring only to those motifs in Trakl's poetry which represent single objects and events. These are often impenetrable. There is, however, a motif which is a representation not simply of one object or event but rather of a process of development in a series of events, as clouded as such a development might be with respect to its chronologically progressing steps. This is the incest theme—perhaps the most striking of Trakl's motifs.

There are several references to an incestuous act scattered throughout the various writings of Trakl. Among the earlier of these is a poem entitled "Blutschuld," a term which can be used as a synonym for "Blutschande" (incest). When the sexual nature of the poem's content is taken into account, the translation of "Blutschuld" as incest is completely in order.

> Es dräut die Nacht am Lager unsrer Küsse.
> Es flüstert wo: Wer nimmt von euch die Schuld?
> Noch bebend von verruchter Wollust Süsse
> Wir beten: Verzeih uns, Maria, in deiner Huld!
>
> Aus Blumenschalen steigen gierige Düfte,
> Umschmeicheln unsere Stirnen bleich von Schuld.
> Ermattend unterm Hauch der schwülen Lüfte
> Wir träumen: Verzeih uns, Maria, in deiner Huld!

> Doch lauter rauscht der Brunnen der Sirenen
> Und dunkler ragt die Sphinx vor unsrer Schuld,
> Dass unsre Herzen sündiger wieder tönen,
> Wir schluchzen: Verzeih uns, Maria, in deiner Huld!
>
> [I: 249]

From this early poem, belonging to the collection of 1909, a very significant detail emerges, one which connects it with the many appearances of the incest theme in Western literature beginning with Sophocles' *Oedipus the King*: the tremendous feeling of guilt associated with incest, quite in keeping with society's revulsion. This traditional revulsion may help explain the overwhelming obsession with feelings of guilt expressed throughout Trakl's work, even in his later poems: e.g., "Gross ist die Schuld des Geborenen" from "Anif" (I: 114) and the aphorism:

> Gefühl in den Augenblicken totenähnlichen Seins: Alle Menschen sind der Liebe wert. Erwachend fühlst du die Bitternis der Welt; darin ist alle deine ungelöste Schuld; dein Gedicht eine unvollkommene Sühne. [I: 463]

Other, more hidden references to incest in some of the earlier poems are as follows:

> Da schimmert aus verworrenen Gestalten
> Ein Frauenbild, umflort von finstrer Trauer,
> Und giesst in mich den Kelch verruchter Schauer.
>
> [I: 221]
>
> Ein schwüler Garten stand die Nacht.
> Wir verschwiegen uns, was uns grauend erfasst.
> Davon sind unsre Herzen erwacht
> Und erlagen unter des Schweigens Last.
>
> Es blühte kein Stern in jener Nacht
> Und niemand war, der für uns bat.
> Ein Dämon nur hat im Dunkel gelacht.
> Seid alle verflucht! Da ward die Tat.
>
> [I: 231]

In later poems the words "Geschwister" and "Schwester" provide more direct indications of incest:

> Im Park erblicken zitternd sich Geschwister.
>
> [I: 29]
>
> Schwester, da ich dich fand an einsamer Lichtung
> Des Waldes und Mittag war und gross das Schweigen des Tiers;

Weisse unter wilder Eiche, und es blühte silbern der Dorn.
Gewaltiges Sterben und die singende Flamme im Herzen.

[I: 141]

All of this raises the rather obvious question: Is there any bio-
graphical basis to the incest theme in Trakl's poetry? Can one deduce
such a relationship from the strange attraction that Trakl felt toward
his younger sister Margarethe? Here the critics are divided, as they
are with regard to a good many features of Trakl's obscure biography.
A definitive statement is especially difficult because of the critics'
proximity in time to the suspected deeds and the fact that those who
might possess information regarding such deeds would very prob-
ably be closely connected to Trakl's family, one of whose members
was still alive as late as 1969. Most of the recent critics, however,
rely on Theodor Spoerri's statement that he possesses indisputable
evidence of an incestuous relationship from a source which he does
not think it prudent to identify.[1] Notable exceptions are Michael
Hamburger (see the Trakl chapter in his *Reason and Energy*)[2] and
apparently even Walther Killy.[3] In the final analysis, however, it is
not important whether such acts actually did occur or whether they
are to be attributed to the neurotically inflated imagination of the
poet. The *theme* of incest clearly does figure significantly in Trakl's
work, and in this the critics do concur unanimously.

"Passion"

The most extensive developments of this theme are to be found in
the *Brenner* version of "Passion" and the prose poems "Traum und
Umnachtung" and "Offenbarung und Untergang." Incest and its con-
sequences are central to these works, and from them emerges some-
thing approximating a narrative description of the incestuous
relationship. The *Brenner* "Passion" follows, quoted in full:

Wenn silbern Orpheus die Laute rührt,
Beklagend ein Totes im Abendgarten—
Wer bist du Ruhendes unter hohen Bäumen?
Es rauscht die Klage das herbstliche Rohr,
Der blaue Teich.   5

Weh, der schmalen Gestalt des Knaben,
Die purpurn erglüht,
Schmerzlicher Mutter, in blauem Mantel
Verhüllend ihre heilige Schmach.

Weh, des Geborenen, dass er stürbe,   10
Eh er die glühende Frucht,
Die bittere der Schuld genossen.

Wen weinst du unter dämmernden Bäumen?
Die Schwester, dunkle Liebe
Eines wilden Geschlechts,   15
Dem auf goldenen Rädern der Tag davonrauscht.

O, dass frömmer die Nacht käme,
Kristus.

Was schweigst du unter schwarzen Bäumen?
Den Sternenfrost des Winters,   20
Gottes Geburt
Und die Hirten an der Krippe von Stroh.

Blaue Monde
Versanken die Augen des Blinden in härener Höhle.

Ein Leichnam suchest du unter grünenden Bäumen   25
Deine Braut,
Die silberne Rose
Schwebend über dem nächtlichen Hügel.

Wandelnd an den schwarzen Ufern
Des Todes,   30
Purpurn erblüht im Herzen die Höllenblume.

Über seufzende Wasser geneigt
Sieh dein Gemahl: Antlitz starrend von Aussatz
Und ihr Haar flattert wild in der Nacht.

Zwei Wölfe im finsteren Wald   35
Mischten wir unser Blut in steinerner Umarmung
Und die Sterne unseres Geschlechts fielen auf uns.

O, der Stachel des Todes.
Verblichene schauen wir uns am Kreuzweg
Und in silbernen Augen   40
Spiegeln sich die schwarzen Schatten unserer Wildnis,
Grässliches Lachen, das unsere Münder zerbrach.

Dornige Stufen sinken ins Dunkel,
Dass röter von kühlen Füssen
Das Blut hinströme auf den steinigen Acker.   45

Auf purpurner Flut
Schaukelt wachend die silberne Schläferin.

Jener aber ward ein schneeiger Baum
Am Beinerhügel,
Ein Wild äugend aus eiternder Wunde,   50
Wieder ein schweigender Stein.

O, die sanfte Sternenstunde
Dieser kristallnen Ruh,
Da in dorniger Kammer
Das aussätzige Antlitz von dir fiel.   55

Nächtlich tönt der Seele einsames Saitenspiel
Dunkler Verzückung
Voll zu den silbernen Füssen der Büsserin
Im verlorenen Garten;
Und an dorniger Hecke knospet der blaue Frühling.   60

Unter dunklen Olivenbäumen
Tritt der rosige Engel
Des Morgens aus dem Grab der Liebenden.

                                        [I: 392–394]

At the first reading the poem seems so hopelessly complex and
obscure as to offer little or no thread of significance on which to base
an interpretation. The figures of Orpheus and Christ seem totally
unrelated. The incestuous relationship between brother and sister is
indicated in the lines: "Die Schwester, dunkle Liebe / Eines wilden
Geschlechts / Dem auf goldenen Rädern der Tag davonrauscht." And
again in: "Zwei Wölfe im finsteren Wald / Mischten wir unser Blut in
steinerner Umarmung / Und die Sterne unseres Geschlechts fielen
auf uns." But who are the various other figures in the poem: the boy
(line 6); the sorrowful mother (line 8); the one born (line 10); the
blind one (line 24); the silver sleeping woman (line 47); and the
penitent woman (line 58)? Who is indicated in the various occur-
rences of the second person singular pronoun (lines 3, 13, 19, 25,
55)? And what about the two neuter adjectival nouns that apparently
refer to persons: "ein Totes" (line 2), "Ruhendes" (line 3)? These
images cannot be easily identified from the immediate context of
their occurrence in the poem. Therefore, rather than concentrating
exclusively on the individual images as Killy does,[4] let us start,
instead, with the assumption that the poem narrates a series of
events. In proceeding from this basic assumption, we can possibly
let more light fall on the various images.

The poem begins with the lament of Orpheus. The singer is
mourning something dead ("ein Totes"), something resting under

high trees ("Ruhendes unter hohen Bäumen"). The word "Totes" is not further identified in the first stanza, but because of the Orpheus legend, the reader would naturally think of Eurydice. The word "Abendgarten" catches the eye. It is echoed by the lost garden ("Im verlorenen Garten") of line 59, which, together with the "Saiten-spiel" of line 56, provides a link between Orpheus and the events described at the end of the poem. The "lost garden" is suggestive of paradise, which, coming near the end of the poem in a context of images signifying the awakening of new life, would be a paradise regained. The "lost garden" with the "penitent woman" calls to mind the garden in which Christ was buried (John 19: 41–42) and Mary Magdalene first discovered the open tomb after the resurrec-tion (John 20: 1). The angel appearing from the grave under dark olive trees (lines 61–63) also belongs within this context. In another poem, "Abendländisches Lied," Trakl uses the word "Abendgarten" in a context which also indicates an association with Christ: "Im Abendgarten, wo vor Zeiten die frommen Jünger gegangen."[5] The "pious disciples" and the "evening garden" here are strongly sugges-tive of the apostles who waited for Christ in the Garden of Geth-semane while he was praying.

The word "Abendgarten" is at least a suggestion of Christ, one strengthened by the use of the same word in a clearer context in "Abenländisches Lied" and all but confirmed by the later, more definite references to Christ in the poem now being analyzed.[6] Thus in the first stanza there is already ambiguity. Orpheus' lament might now be construed as concerning the dead Christ as well as Eurydice. When Killy maintains, therefore, that all references to Christ have been eliminated from the condensed final version of the poem (I: 125), except possibly the words "Stille Nacht,"[7] he overlooks not only the word "Büsserin" but also the word "Abendgarten," both of which are retained from the Brenner version and both of which point, if not to Christ, then at least to the Christian realm.

In the second stanza the lament continues and the ambiguity in-creases. Now it appears that the boy is being mourned; in the follow-ing stanza he is called the one born ("der Geborene"), an ominous word in Trakl's vocabulary, one generally used in contrast to the innocence of the unborn ("der Ungeborene"). The boy is passion-ately inflamed ("purpurn erglüht"), the object of his passions appear-ing in line 14: "Die Schwester."[8] The "sorrowful mother" with her blue cloak and holy shame is suggestive of Christ's mother at the crucifixion. But she is also the mother of the boy who is implicated sexually with his sister, a striking example of Trakl's interweaving of the sacred and scandalous. There is an indication in the line "Verhüllend ihre heilige Schmach" that the mother knows of her children's sin and that from this her shame arises. In a telling passage from "Traum und Umnachtung," the reader gains the impression that the boy has been caught in the act by his mother:

> Sein Haupt verbrannte Lüge and Unzucht in dämmernden Zimmern. Das blaue Rauschen eines Frauengewandes liess ihn zur Säule erstarren und in der Tür stand die nächtige Gestalt seiner Mutter. [I: 148]

Thus, Orpheus' lament concerns the boy, who can also be associated with the dead one of lines 2 and 3 ("ein Totes," "Ruhendes"). Lines 10 to 12 (". . . dass er stürbe, / Eh er die glühende Frucht, / Die bittere der Schuld genossen") express a wish that the boy die before falling into sin and guilt. Line 25 then definitely identifies him as a corpse ("Ein Leichnam"). It can be assumed, therefore, that the boy is dead already, as a result of his sin. Although the words "dass er stürbe" express a wish for the future, this future time must be measured from the time of birth ("Weh, des Geborenen, dass er stürbe") and considered as prior to the eating of the fruit of guilt and therefore also to the lament of Orpheus. This wish is not fulfilled; the boy does live to eat the forbidden fruit but dies thereafter to be lamented by Orpheus.

In the next stanza there is another intermingling of roles. The boy mourned by Orpheus takes up the lament and directs it toward his sister, who, likewise, enters into association with the dead one in the evening garden under the trees of lines 2 and 3. The "du" in the question of line 13 ("Wen weinst du unter dämmernden Bäumen?") can be none other than the guilty boy, as the answer of the following line, "Die Schwester," confirms. This is the second time that the "du" form appears in the poem; and while the first occurrence in line 3 ("Wer bist du Ruhendes unter hohen Bäumen?") is not so clearly identifiable (referring, as we have seen, to Eurydice, Christ, the boy, and finally the sister), the second occurrence leaves little doubt as to its meaning.[9]

The scene abruptly changes now to focus on the figure of Christ. Is this just another example of Trakl's kaleidoscopic technique, the abrupt juxtaposition of disconnected images; or is there a unifying center around which these seemingly antithetical images may be grouped? Here the transition to Christ is not altogether as abrupt as it may, at first, seem. If the foregoing determination of the significance of the evening garden and the sorrowful mother in the blue cloak is correct, these images would already have prepared the way for the appearance of Christ. But more important, in accord with the procedure of this interpretation, we should ask what takes place from lines 17 to 22. The answer is simple: "Gottes Geburt," the nativity of Christ, which can be contrasted with the other birth alluded to in line 10 ("des Geborenen"), the one doomed to lead to guilt and death. The happier birth presages the conclusion of the poem with its strong indications of a new birth, a resurrection.

The next two lines introduce a blind one ("der Blinde") whose eyes apparently sink in their hairy sockets. The "härene Höhle" could refer to eye sockets (Augenhöhlen) surrounded with hair. In a religious sense, however, the word "hären" evokes the hair shirt of the penitent and thus points ahead to lines 43–45 and 52–55, where the penitential mood is more strongly implied (see also "Büsserin" in line 58).[10] The raising the lowering of the eyes or eyelids is one of the recurring motifs in Trakl's poetry and is usually associated with death: e.g., the conclusion of "Helian"—"Da der Enkel in sanfter Umnachtung / Einsam dem dunkleren Ende nachsinnt, / Der stille Gott die blauen Lider über ihn senkt" (I: 73); and also in "Sebastian im Traum"—"Ein zarter Leichnam stille im Dunkel der Kammer lag / Und jener die kalten Lider über ihn aufhob" (I: 88).

The next stanza, lines 25–28, describes the search for the sister. "Ein Leichnam" is in apposition to "du" and refers to the boy's condition, just as in the preceding stanza "Blaue Monde," also coming at the beginning of a sentence, is in apposition to "die Augen." These are examples of one of Trakl's peculiar syntactical devices which will be considered in depth in Chapter 7. There have been indications, however, in previous lines (see 1–3 and 13–14) that the sister is also dead.

By the end of the first section of the poem, the reader is left with a strong impression of an all-encompassing death deriving in some mysterious way from an incestuous act. But there are also some faint indications, ensuing from the reference to Christ's birth, of the possible renewal of life. The variants for this poem in the critical edition show that the poet had written an earlier version of lines 25–28 which clearly anticipates the ending of the poem and which he subsequently rejected for use at this particular stage:

> Den Tod erleidend unter grünenden Bäumen,
> Immer singt die Rose

In Nacht und steinernem Grab die Auferstehung,
Morgen, der rosig hervorgeht.

[II: 220]

At the beginning of the second section of the *Brenner* version, which is separated from the first section by a wider space between the stanzas, the boy-Orpheus continues his search for his sister-Eurydice. He is described as still under the sway of his passions: "Purpurn erblüht im Herzen die Höllenblume." In the next stanza one finds another motif that occurs frequently in Trakl's poetry: the narcissistic reflection in a mirrorlike surface. The boy, bent over the sighing waters, sees apparently not his own reflection but his sister's, covered with a leprous growth. The "Gemahl" of line 33 is a neuter noun substituting in poetic usage for "Gemahlin," and the words "ihr Haar" of line 34 leave no doubt that the reflection is feminine. The sister takes on the boy's own image, a point which will be expanded upon later. For now it will be sufficient to cite two passages from "Traum und Umnachtung" in which this motif is more clearly presented: "Aus blauem Spiegel trat die schmale Gestalt der Schwester und er stürzte wie tot ins Dunkel" (I: 147); and "Hass verbrannte sein Herz, Wollust, da er im grünenden Sommergarten dem schweigenden Kind Gewalt tat, in dem strahlenden sein umnachtetes Antlitz erkannte" (I: 148).

The next stanza shifts to the past tense and metaphorically describes the incest act itself. Here also the "du" form, which has figured prominently in the poem from the very beginning, gives way abruptly to the more autobiographical "wir." In the final version of the poem, Trakl changes this all too personal reference from the first person to the third person: "Unter finsteren Tannen / Mischten zwei Wölfe ihr Blut" (I: 125) rather than "Zwei Wölfe im finsteren Wald / Mischten wir unser Blut in steinerner Umarmung." Such a modification is indicative of Trakl's tendency, in his later works, to suppress the person of the poet as completely as possible within the poem. Indeed, in a letter to his friend Erhard Buschbeck in late 1911 he writes of a revised poem:

> Es ist umso viel besser als das ursprüngliche als es nun unpersönlich ist, und zum Bersten voll von Bewegung und Gesichten.
> Ich bin überzeugt, dass es Dir in dieser universellen Form und Art mehr sagen und bedeuten wird, denn in der begrenzt persönlichen des ersten Entwurfes. [I: 485]

This excerpt makes it clear that the critic who understands the many allusions to incest and sister merely as autobiographical references is making a mistake; in their "universal form" these allusions tell far more, as Trakl himself indicates.

"Zwei Wölfe" is in apposition to "wir." The wolf appears in Trakl's works with its usual connotation as a creature of passion and destruction. "Ein Wolf zerriss das Erstgeborene" we read in "Traum und Umnachtung" (I: 149). In another passage of the same prose poem the incestuous boy is described as a wolf: "Aber in dunkler Höhle verbrachte er seine Tage, log und stahl und verbarg sich, ein flammender Wolf, vor dem weissen Antlitz der Mutter" (I: 147). The word "Blut" (line 36) also fits in well with the incest theme if one recalls that in German incest is "Blutschande," or in Trakl's vocabulary, "Blutschuld." Thus the "mixing of the blood" is an extremely appropriate metaphor for the incest act. Blood also appears later in the poem, in line 45, where it is spilt upon a stony field, as if in expiation for the previous sin.

In the next stanza (lines 38–42) a meeting between the brother and sister takes place, signficantly, at a crossroads ("Kreuzweg"), a typically ambivalent image which could imply the way of the cross. The word "Kreuz" appears several times in Trakl's poetry and carries with it the connotation of an instrument of suffering, the Christian cross (e.g., "Blutend Kreuz im Sterngefunkel" [I: 417]). Thus it would refer ahead to the next stanza, where the suffering and expiation of the two lovers are clearly indicated. But the "Kreuzweg" as crossroads is traditionally an evil place and thus sets the mood for the next three lines with their almost orgiastic nihilism. The stanza begins with an evocation of the thorn of death ("Stachel des Todes"); the lovers are called "Verblichene," another word connoting death. It has already been established that the lovers are now dead and that their death probably results from the incest act, but the reader senses also that, even after death, they continue to suffer and be plagued by their passions. Indeed this "Passion," in the ambivalent sense of that word, could go on forever (cf. "Dass nimmer der dornige Stachel ablasse vom verwesenden Leib" [I: 121]). In his Trakl interpretation Heinrich Goldmann emphasizes the phallic as well as the deathly quality of words like "Stachel" and "Dorn."[11] This ambivalence is also contained in the following sentence from "Offenbarung und Untergang": "Aus verwesender Bläue trat die bleiche Gestalt der Schwester und also sprach ihr blutender Mund: Stich schwarzer Dorn" (I: 168).

In the course of this meeting at the crossroads another reflection takes place. Just as the lovers share the same blood, so now they share the same shame and despair, as shown in the mutual reflection of their eyes. This second reflection is of the same nature as that of lines 32–34, except that now the eyes of the lovers take over the function of the water. The significance of the color "silbern" used to describe the eyes is difficult to determine. Here the immediate context prevents it from taking on the positive value of indicating the possible beginning of a transformation process. The value assigned by the interpreter to individual recurring words, especially color adjectives which often appear to be used quite arbitrarily by the poet, in Killy's sense as "Chiffren," must always depend at least in part on the context in which they are used. It is by failing to observe this criterion that Lachmann frequently arrives at his all too obvious manipulations of the text. Again it must be stressed that it is not the individual images which are of prime importance to the present interpretation, but rather the totality of the developments taking place within the poem. Single words which apparently do not fit into a given context in this poem can either point ahead or point back to other stages of the poem, thus helping to achieve the effect of an intermingling of stages. It would be wrong, therefore, to assume that their use is completely arbitrary when seen from the total perspective of the poem.

In the next stanza (lines 43–45) there are definite signs of an expiation of guilt through suffering. It cannot be said, however, that expiation begins with this stanza; there have been earlier indications of such a process. The very fact that the brother and sister appear dead from the beginning of the poem shows at least in part an atonement for their deed. The first line of this stanza speaks of a descent by thorny steps into the darkness. Besides the possible association of "thorny steps" with Christ's crown of thorns, there is also the suggestion of a descent into a tomb, an impression strengthened by the words "dornige Kammer" in line 54 and the reference at the end of the poem to the grave of the lovers. There are many instances of such descending motion in Trakl's poetry: the lowering of the eyelids, the inclining of the head, the dropping of the dew in the realm of inanimate nature, as well as other instances of humans descending stairs. In the last case the atmosphere of death and the grave is quite often present, as in a variant of the ending of "Helian" which shows some similarity to line 43 of "Passion." After the line "Der stille Gott die blauen Lider über ihn senkt," Trakl had originally planned to continue with: "jener über zerbrochene Stufen schweigend ins Dunkel hinabsteigt" (II: 132).

The last stanza of this section (lines 46–47) refers specifically to the sister in the form of the silver sleeping woman. The word "Schläferin" appears several times in Trakl's works. In an untitled drama fragment from early 1914 which bears many similarities to "Offenbarung und Untergang," Johanna, the sister, is described as a dark sleeping woman ("finstere Schläferin" [I: 458]). Her appearance is heralded by the stage direction: "sleep walking" ("traumwandelnd" [I: 459]). Her murderer, Kermor, appears initially in the same condition and awakens only after seeing her.

It is useful to pursue here a biographical connection. We know that Trakl was addicted to drugs and introduced his sister to their use, thus making an addict out of her. The extent of her addiction is exposed by her letter to Trakl's friend Buschbeck in which she asks for his help in procuring opium.[12] Trakl execrates the addiction to drugs in one of his poems entitled "Der Schlaf": "Verflucht ihr dunklen Gifte, / Weisser Schlaf!" (I: 156).[13] The drug addiction of his sister helps to explain the apparently antithetical juxtaposition in line 47 of "wachend" and "Schläferin," perhaps an indication of a drugged sleep, not a real sleep. The "purple flood" of line 46 suggests the blood of the preceding stanza which flows from the feet of the two penitents. It also evokes the Stygian waters of the underworld and thus the shade of Eurydice following her lover toward a possible release. Here again there is an instance of the interweaving of the Orphic and the Christian worlds.

The entire last section of the poem (lines 48–63) describes the transformation which has taken place in the lovers. In the first stanza (lines 48–51) three objects are mentioned: a tree, an animal, a stone, all of which appear to be stages in a transformation undergone by the brother, the "Jener" of line 48. There is a similar metamorphosis much more succinctly described in the prose poem "Verwandlung des Bösen": "Du auf verfallenen Stufen: Baum, Stern, Stein! Du, ein blaues Tier, das leise zittert" (I: 97). It is interesting to note that the German Romanticist Novalis, whom Trakl honored with a poem, "An Novalis" (I: 324–326), and with several references to the "blaue Blume" in his poetry, lets his hero, Heinrich von Ofterdingen, undergo such a metamorphosis in stages in his notes for the continuation of the second part of the novel. Tieck reports as follows:

> Heinrich pflückt die blaue Blume . . . und wird ein Stein. "Edda (die blaue Blume, die Morgenländerin, Mathilde) opfert sich an dem Steine, er verwandelt sich in einen klingenden Baum. Cyane haut den Baum um, und verbrennt sich mit ihm, er wird ein goldner Widder. Edda, Mathilde muss ihn opfern. Er wird wieder ein Mensch."[14]

There is an important difference, however, between Heinrich's metamorphosis and that of the boy in Trakl's poem. There is an inner logic to the account of Novalis, namely the progression to the human level through, first, the inorganic level ("Stein") and then the plant and animal levels ("Baum," "Widder") of creation. This logic is lacking in Trakl's account, unless one sees in the fact that "Stein" is mentioned last a transformation removing the boy ultimately farthest from the human sphere. Thus far, we have established only that a transformation has taken place. Nothing definite can yet be said about the nature of this transformation.

The next stanza (lines 52–55) seems to deal with the transformation of the sister. It takes place in a thorny chamber (line 54) which suggests a tomb at the end of the thorny steps. Here the leprous countenance, first mentioned in line 33, falls from her. The "dir" of line 55 is apparently the only time in the poem that a second person singular pronoun refers exclusively to the sister. It has been noted that the previous uses of this form refer chiefly to the boy. But if the foregoing interpretation of the reflection motif (lines 32–34) is correct, then "dir" refers also to the boy. His countenance is also purified, just as it is both his sister's and his own image that he sees reflected in the sighing waters. In other words, in the perplexing imagery and language of the poem the boy is his sister.

The next stanza (lines 56–60) makes mention of the "lonely string music of the soul," again evoking the figure of Orpheus the musician—here near the end of the poem. One could therefore speak of a circular movement in this poem, although spiral would be a better term since the poem ends on a higher note than it begins. The lament of Orpheus concludes in a joyous message of resurrection. The string music is played not for Eurydice, but at the feet of the penitent woman ("die Büsserin"). The word "Büsserin" evokes the figure of Mary Magdalene, especially in the light of the last stanza where the angel appears from the grave. (Trakl, it should be noted, wrote an early prose work in dialogue form entitled "Maria Magdalena," in which there is a description of a very sensuous woman who later devoted herself completely to Christ [I: 195–198]). The New Testament relates how, at their first meeting, Mary Magdalene washed the feet of Christ. In Trakl's "Passion," however, the penitent woman is not at the Master's feet; rather the string music is played at her feet. Thus she, in a way, has become a kind of Christ figure herself. It has already been shown how Orpheus merges with Christ and with the boy and how the boy merges with his sister. Now the circle becomes complete as the sister is linked to Christ and to Orpheus through

Eurydice (the "Schläferin" of line 47). Thus, in spite of what can be called the disconnected, illogical images in this poem and elsewhere in Trakl's poetry, the conclusion is inescapable that at least the human figures of this poem are intimately linked.

The last stanza contains the motif of the resurrection—by no means its only appearance in Trakl's poetry.[15] It is prefigured in the last line of the preceding stanza where spring blossoms appear on the thorny hedge, an image indicating a transformation also of the thorn of death ("der Stachel des Todes") of line 38. At the end of the poem, an angel emerges from a tomb, highly suggestive of the empty tomb of Christ on Easter morning. The angel is another of the ambiguous figures in Trakl's writings, sometimes appearing as the fallen angel as in the poem "Geburt" (I: 115) and even as Lucifer himself in the poem "An Luzifer" (I: 335). Trakl's angel is not like Rilke's angel, a symbol with a distinctly defined significance.[16] It must be noted also that the angel of line 62 steps not from Christ's tomb but from the tomb of the incestuous pair, who are now, for the first time in the poem, called lovers. The angel could, therefore, represent a being produced by the union of these lovers. The angel is described as rosy ("rosig"), one of the very few color designations in Trakl's poetry whose significance is fairly unambiguous.[17] Rosy has a more concrete function as the color of the dawning day, thus suggesting a renewal of life,[18] and has, therefore, a generally optimistic connotation in Trakl's poetry.[19]

Before I summarize, a few remarks are in order about the flow of time in this poem. A number of critics have noted that fall and winter as well as evening and night, the declining times of the year and day respectively, predominate in Trakl's poetry. In many of the poems there is also a definite progression of time to be noted: for instance, in "Jahr" (I: 138) the seasons are associated with the stages of human life; in "Frühling der Seele" (I: 141–142) and "Die Sonne" (I: 134) there is a movement from morning to evening. Many of the poems show a progression from evening to night (e.g., "De profundis" [I: 46], "Unterwegs" [I: 81], "Untergang" [I: 116], "Geistliche Dämmerung" [I: 118], and "Sommer" [I: 136]). The poem under consideration proceeds in a similar manner from evening to night but ends with the morning. In lines 1–16 the mood of the evening dominates (e.g, "Abendgarten" [line 2], "unter dämmernden Bäumen" [line 13], "Dem auf goldenen Rädern der Tag davonrauscht" [line 16]). From line 17 on, the mood of night becomes predominant (e.g., "O, dass frömmer die Nacht käme" [line 17], "über dem nächtlichen Hügel" [line 28], "in der Nacht" [line 34], and "Nächtlich tönt" [line

56]).[20] Finally, in the last stanza morning arrives ("Des Morgens" [line 63]), the morning of resurrection.

In the course of the foregoing analysis, a certain pattern of development in this poem has been seen to emerge. Against this background, several of the otherwise hopelessly obscure images (i.e., the human figures) have taken on a coherent significance. The important stages of this development are, without regard to the order of their appearance, as follows: (1) the incest act; (2) death (3) suffering and expiation; (4) purification and transformation culminating in an indication of new life. The incest act leads not only to the shame of the mother and the bitter fruit of guilt but also to the death of brother and sister. The atmosphere of death predominates in the poem from the very beginning. In the realm of death the boy appears as Orpheus and his sister as Eurydice (the "Schläferin"). In this realm, the "passion" of the incestuous pair continues, but now the emphasis is on passion as suffering, thus calling to mind the suffering and death of Christ (the evening garden, the way of the cross, the thorny steps, the blood flowing from feet onto the stony field, the hill of bones, and the penitent woman). Orpheus mourns the death not only of the boy and his sister but also of Christ. Orphic music ("Saitenspiel") also ushers in the final stage of the poem, the rebirth, which is anticipated by the stanza dealing with the birth of Christ earlier in the poem. The Orphic music is played for the penitent woman who thus exchanges roles with Eurydice. But since it is played at her *feet*, she also exchanges roles with Christ, at whose feet the penitent woman is traditionally pictured. These developments can be illustrated in the following way: sister = Eurydice = penitent woman = Christ, just as boy = Orpheus = Christ. The different figures are really personifications of the various stages of one and the same process— the process that leads from incest through death and expiation to a divine rebirth. These stages with their corresponding figures are as follows: (1) incest—the boy and his sister; (2) death—Orpheus and Eurydice; (3) and (4) expiation and transformation—Christ and the penitent woman.

After careful scrutiny, many of the various elements of this poem do, indeed, fit together to form a meaningful whole. Contrary to the opinion of Killy, they do "make sense." It is true that the poem's progression from one step to the other is difficult to determine. The individual images should therefore be examined not only in their immediate context but with constant reference to the poem as a whole as well as to the entire corpus of Trakl's poetry, which, as Killy himself argues, constitutes one poem. The images themselves are not autonomous, but serve to illuminate the aforementioned process. In the remainder of Part I, it will become clear that the most important detail of this process is the union of brother and sister expressed in the words: "Über seufzende Wasser geneigt / Sieh dein Gemahl. . . ." It is here that the sameness of brother and sister—the ultimate goal of their transformation—first comes to light.

Trakl trimmed the length of the final version of the poem (I: 125), the one appearing in the edition *Sebastian im Traum* published shortly after the poet's death, from sixty-three lines to twenty-nine lines. Instead of three large sections encompassing eighteen stanzas, there are now only three longer stanzas. The stanzas referring to Christ's birth are compressed into two words at the end of the first stanza: "Stille Nacht." The suggestion of expiation is limited to a self-destructive wish expressed at the end of the second stanza, "Dass endlich zerbräche das kühle Haupt!" and the words "Abend-garten" and "Büsserin" retained from the earlier version. All reference to a possible resurrection is omitted from the end of the poem which now reads:

> Oder es tönte dunkler Verzückung
> Voll das Saitenspiel
> Zu den kühlen Füssen der Büsserin
> In der steinernen Stadt.

[I: 125]

This is not, however, an entirely pessimistic ending, especially when compared with the ending of the preceding stanza. The last line with its stony city does, to be sure, give the impression of heaviness, of hopelessness. But if one bears in mind the power of Orphic music ("das Saitenspiel") to transform stones, then the notion of transformation will not seem entirely absent from the last stanza. The first lines of this stanza ("Denn immer folgt, ein blaues Wild, / Ein Äugendes unter dämmernden Bäumen, / Dieser dunkleren Pfaden") represent a condensation of lines 48–51 of the earlier version, lines describing the transformation of the boy. Thus Trakl tends to render his images inscrutable by condensing and compressing them in the process of revision until only fleeting impressions of an original context are left (see also the above cited "Stille Nacht"). For this reason, among others, his poetry has been occasionally referred to as "hermetic": that is, its meaning is supposed to be understandable only to the initiate or to the poet himself.[21]

The original, more extensive version of "Passion," however, can no longer be considered as impenetrable, nor can, in the light of the foregoing interpretation, the following untitled poem, written sometime during the summer of 1913 and published for the first time in the critical edition. The reader will note that it contains much the same development of theme and concluding motif as "Passion":

> Die blaue Nacht ist sanft auf unsren Stirnen aufgegangen.
> Leise berühren sich unsre verwesten Hände
> Süsse Braut!
>
> Bleich ward unser Antlitz, mondene Perlen
> Verschmolzen in grünem Weihergrund.
> Versteinerte schauen wir unsre Sterne.
>
> O Schmerzliches! Schuldige wandeln im Garten
> In wilder Umarmung die Schatten,
> Dass in gewaltigem Zorn Baum und Tier über sie sank.
>
> Sanfte Harmonien, da wir in kristallnen Wogen
> Fahren durch die stille Nacht
> Ein rosiger Engel aus den Gräbern der Liebenden tritt.
>
> [I: 313]

The Last Prose Poems

The theme of incest is also central to the two prose poems "Traum und Umnachtung" and "Offenbarung und Untergang." I have isolated below those passages which refer more directly to the incest act and its consequences or which bear resemblance to "Passion":

> Traum und Umnachtung
>
> [I: 147–150]

Am Abend ward zum Greis der Vater; in dunklen Zimmern versteinerte das Antlitz der Mutter und auf dem Knaben lastete der Fluch des entarteten Geschlechts. Manchmal erinnerte er sich seiner Kindheit, erfüllt von Krankheit, Schrecken und Finsternis, verschwiegener Spiele im Sternengarten, oder dass er die Ratten fütterte im dämmernden Hof. Aus blauem Spiegel trat die schmale Gestalt der Schwester und er stürzte wie tot ins Dunkel. [Lines 1–7][22]

Hass verbrannte sein Herz, Wollust, da er im grünenden Sommergarten dem schweigenden Kind Gewalt tat, in dem strahlenden sein umnachtetes Antlitz erkannte. Weh, des Abends am Fenster, da aus purpurnen Blumen, ein gräulich Gerippe, der Tod trat. [Lines 30–33]

Sein Haupt verbrannte Lüge und Unzucht in dämmernden Zimmern. Das blaue Rauschen eines Frauengewandes liess ihn zur Säule erstarren und in der Tür stand die nächtige Gestalt seiner Mutter. [Lines 35–37]

Fiebernd sass er auf der eisigen Stiege, rasend gen Gott, dass er stürbe. O, das graue Antlitz des Schreckens, da er die runden Augen über einer Taube zerschnittener Kehle aufhob. [Lines 50–52]

In einem verödeten Durchhaus erschien ihm starrend von Unrat seine blutende Gestalt. [Lines 58–59]

Aber da er Glühendes sinnend den herbstlichen Fluss hinabging unter kahlen Bäumen hin, erschien in härenem Mantel ihm, ein flammender Dämon, die Schwester. Beim Erwachen erloschen zu ihren Häuptern die Sterne. [Lines 63–65]

Also fand er im Dornenbusch die weisse Gestalt des Kindes, blutend nach dem Mantel seines Bräutigams. [Lines 79–80]

Nachtlang wohnte er in kristallener Höhle und der Aussatz wuchs silbern auf seiner Stirne. [Lines 82–83]

Bitter ist der Tod, die Kost der Schuldbeladenen; in dem braunen Geäst des Stamms zerfielen grinsend die irdenen Gesichter. [Lines 95–97]

Weh der steinernen Augen der Schwester, da beim Mahle ihr Wahnsinn auf die nächtige Stirne des Bruders trat, . . . [Lines 109–110]

Purpurne Wolke umwölkte sein Haupt, dass er schweigend über sein eigenes Blut und Bildnis herfiel, ein mondenes Antlitz; steinern ins Leere hinsank, da in zerbrochenem Spiegel, ein sterbender Jüngling, die Schwester erschien; die Nacht das verfluchte Geschlecht verschlang. [Lines 120–123]

Obviously these lines, charged, as they are, with so much dramatic tension and emotional energy, do not give anything resembling a coherent, realistic account of the incest act. They present instead an overwhelmingly depressing picture in which the horror of the act and its deathly consequences are highlighted. There is very little indication of possible transformation, at least thus far. The situation changes somewhat in "Offenbarung und Untergang" (I: 168–170).

Seltsam sind die nächtigen Pfade des Menschen. Da ich nachtwandelnd an steinernen Zimmern hinging und es brannte in jedem ein stilles Lämpchen, ein kupferner Leuchter, und da ich frierend aufs Lager hinsank, stand zu Häupten wieder der schwarze Schatten der Fremdlingin und schweigend verbarg ich das Antlitz in den langsamen Händen. [Lines 1–6]

Leise trat aus kalkiger Mauer ein unsägliches Antlitz—ein sterbender
Jüngling—die Schönheit eines heimkehrenden Geschlechts. [Lines
12–13]

Schweigend sass ich in verlassener Schenke unter verrauchtem Holz-
gebälk und einsam beim Wein; ein strahlender Leichnam über ein
Dunkles geneigt und es lag ein totes Lamm zu meinen Füssen. Aus
verwesender Bläue trat die bleiche Gestalt der Schwester und also
sprach ihr blutender Mund: Stich schwarzer Dorn. Ach noch tönen
von wilden Gewittern die silbernen Arme mir. Fliesse Blut von den
mondenen Füssen, blühend auf nächtigen Pfaden, darüber schreiend
die Ratte huscht. [Lines 16–22]

. . . und leise rann aus silberner Wunde der Schwester das Blut und
fiel ein feuriger Regen auf mich. [Lines 32–33]

Aber da ich den Felsenpfad hinabstieg, ergriff mich der Wahnsinn
und ich schrie laut in der Nacht; und da ich mit silbernen Fingern
mich über die schweigenden Wasser bog, sah ich dass mich mein
Antlitz verlassen. Und die weisse Stimme sprach zu mir: Töte dich!
Seufzend erhob sich eines Knaben Schatten in mir und sah mich
strahlend aus kristallnen Augen an, dass ich weinend unter den
Bäumen hinsank, dem gewaltigen Sternengewölbe. [Lines 42–47]

Aber leise kommst du in der Nacht, da ich wachend am Hügel lag,
oder rasend im Frühlingsgewitter; und schwärzer immer umwölkt die
Schwermut das abgeschiedene Haupt, erschrecken schaurige Blitze
die nächtige Seele, zerreissen deine Hände die atemlose Brust mir.

Da ich in den dämmernden Garten ging, und es war die schwarze
Gestalt des Bösen von mir gewichen, umfing mich die hyazinthene
Stille der Nacht; und ich fuhr auf gebogenem Kahn über den ruhen-
den Weiher und süsser Frieden rührte die versteinerte Stirne mir.
Sprachlos lag ich unter den alten Weiden und es war der blaue Him-
mel hoch über mir und voll von Sternen; und da ich anschauend
hinstarb, starben Angst und der Schmerzen tiefster in mir; und es hob
sich der blaue Schatten des Knaben strahlend im Dunkel, sanfter
Gesang; hob sich auf mondenen Flügeln über die grünenden Wipfel,
kristallene Klippen das weisse Antlitz der Schwester.

Mit silbernen Sohlen stieg ich die dornigen Stufen hinab und ich trat
ins kalkgetünchte Gemach. Stille brannte ein Leuchter darin und ich
verbarg in purpurnen Linnen schweigend das Haupt; und es warf die
Erde einen kindlichen Leichnam aus, ein mondenes Gebilde, das
langsam aus meinem Schatten trat, mit zerbrochenen Armen
steinerne Stürze hinabsank, flockiger Schnee. [Lines 51–68]

These passages, likewise, do not represent the usual kind of narra-
tive. There is no continuity at all, either within the passages or from

passage to passage. Trakl renders the account in a completely sur-
realistic manner, without adhering to the laws of logic. The narrator
tells of his death in the last passage quoted, and yet the impression
from the very beginning of "Traum und Umnachtung" is that he is
either dead or in a deathlike state. In an unquoted passage from
"Traum und Umnachtung" he describes himself as the shadow of a
dead man ("der Schatten des Toten" [line 106]); and in the quoted
lines 16–22 from "Offenbarung und Untergang" he calls himself a
radiant corpse ("ein strahlender Leichnam"). "Offenbarung und Un-
tergang" is nevertheless different from the previous prose poem. The
hopelessness which surrounds the incest act there is now replaced
in at least a few of the passages by a kind of buoyancy, an intimation
of release and fulfillment. For a striking example of this change of
mood, notice the words at the end of "Traum und Umnachtung"
which contain a reference to the sister as a dying young man. In
"Offenbarung und Untergang" this reference appears again (lines
12–13), but in a completely different context. Here these words are
appended: "die Schönheit eines heimkehrenden Geschlechts." Even
in such utterances of "Offenbarung und Untergang" as the words of
the sister—"Stich schwarzer Dorn." and "Töte dich!"—the impres-
sion is not merely one of murderous or suicidal tendencies given free
rein but, in the light of what follows, an atonement for the oppres-
sive guilt weighing on the pair. When compared with "Passion," the
first prose poem shows more of the incest and death stages; the
second contains the expiation and transformation stages. Thus the
two prose poems are linked together not only in theme but in the
continuity of the stages of this theme.

Many critics have pointed out that toward the end of his life,
Trakl's poetry tended to manifest a growing state of despair. This is
certainly not true in respect to his prose poems. "Traum und Um-
nachtung" was written in the beginning of 1914 and "Offenbarung
und Untergang" in May of the same year (see II: 265, 312), yet the
latter is definitely more optimistic in tone. These prose poems have
not received much attention in critical works. Even Lachmann treats
them in a rather cursory manner, after first amending them by writ-
ing them in what he considers to be their natural verse.[23] An article
by Herbert Lindenberger attempts to deal more thoroughly with
these poems, but not from the perspective of the present interpreta-
tion.[24]

In "Traum und Umnachtung" Trakl makes a number of references
to the sameness of brother and sister. Both at the beginning and the
end of the poem the sister appears in a mirror. Although it is not

explicitly stated that she is the boy's reflection, there can be little doubt of this, especially since the same motif occurs in "Passion," where the water has the properties of the mirror. In lines 58–59 of the prose poem the boy sees his own bloody figure, this time caked with refuse ("starrend von Unrat"—cf. the sister in the reflection motif of "Passion": "starrend von Aussatz"). Lines 30–33 contain an unmistakable indication of their sameness in the fact that the boy recognizes his own image in the child to whom he does violence (". . . Wollust, da er im grünenden Sommergarten dem schweigenden Kind Gewalt tat, in dem strahlenden sein umnachtetes Antlitz erkannte"). It is interesting to note that the setting of this obvious reference to a sexual encounter is the "Sommergarten." This echoes the concealed games in the starry garden ("verschwiegene Spiele im Sternengarten" [line 5]). The transformation at the end of "Offenbarung und Untergang" also occurs in a garden, this time a twilight garden. This brings to mind the important role the garden plays in "Passion" as the place of Orpheus' lament and the transformation of the lovers.[25]

Also, as in "Passion," the mother is mentioned. Lines 35–37 of "Traum und Umnachtung" indicate that the mother had discovered her children's secret ("Sein Haupt verbrannte Lüge und Unzucht in dämmernden Zimmern. Das blaue Rauschen eines Frauengewandes liess ihn zur Säule erstarren und in der Tür stand die nächtige Gestalt seiner Mutter"). It soon becomes clear that death is the consequence of their act (lines 30–33 and especially lines 95–96: "Bitter ist der Tod, die Kost der Schuldbeladenen;"). The sister's role in this death is ambivalent, as is her significance as an independent figure for Trakl's poetry in general. Sometimes she appears as the innocent victim, and sometimes she herself is the instrument of death. For the former instance the following examples will serve as illustrations: In "Traum und Umnachtung" she appears as the dove with the slit throat (lines 51–52) and the bloody child reaching for the cloak of her bridegroom (lines 79–80); in "Offenbarung und Untergang" she is the dead lamb at the feet of the poet (lines 17–18). But she can also appear in a threatening aspect, as in "Traum und Umnachtung," lines 6–7 ("Aus blauem Spiegel trat die schmale Gestalt der Schwester und er stürzte wie tot ins Dunkel"). In the same poem she is the flaming demon in the hair-cloak (lines 63–65) and she infects the brother with her insanity (lines 109–110). In "Offenbarung und Untergang" she has, at times, the same threatening aspect: "der schwarze Schatten der Fremdlingin" (line 5), "Stich schwarzer Dorn" (lines 19–20), "Töte dich!" (line 45), and ". . . zerreissen deine

Hände die atemlose Brust mir" (lines 53–54). But she also appears to
lead the brother toward expiation: "Fliesse Blut von den mondenen
Füssen," (lines 20–21), an image similar to lines 44–45 of "Passion,"
and ". . . leise rann aus silberner Wunde der Schwester das Blut und
fiel ein feuriger Regen auf mich" (lines 32–33). This expiation can-
not, of course, be understood in an orthodox Christian sense. It is
rather a wild, almost orgiastic wish for self-destruction; but it is
prompted by an intense feeling of guilt. Self-destruction does not
necessarily mean annihilation for Trakl. It seems here rather to be
the gateway to a kind of transfiguration, a new birth in which both
brother and sister participate. In lines 45–47 of "Offenbarung und
Untergang" a different kind of boy is depicted as arising ("erhob
sich") *within* the incestuous brother. This boy who looks radiantly at
the poet out of crystal eyes is, like the boy "Elis," that part of the poet
which does not seem to share in his guilt. In the penultimate para-
graph of "Offenbarung und Untergang" both the boy and the sister,
reflections of each other, arise in transfiguration.

The last paragraph, however, alludes to another kind of birth.
There is the same descent by thorny steps to an underground cham-
ber as in "Passion" and the variant to the ending of "Helian" (see
p. 19). A light burns in this chamber like the light in the stony rooms
at the beginning of the prose poem,[26] thus linking the end to the
beginning in a manner similar to what occurs in both "Passion" and
"Traum and Umnachtung" (see pp. 21, 28). The earth casts out a
child's corpse which emerges from the shadow of the poet and seems
to disintegrate as flaky snow. This could suggest the purification of
the poet and thus be part of the transformation stage. Another in-
terpretation is possible, however. One can consider the last para-
graph as parallel to the end of the preceding one and not a further
development from it. As if seeking to achieve greater ambiguity,
Trakl frequently prefaces an image following another with the word
"oder" (see ending of final version of "Passion"). Although not using
this device here, perhaps the poet wishes to indicate two pos-
sibilities of birth: the first one a rebirth of transfiguration and the
second a stillbirth, a birth into death. The motif of birth occurs
elsewhere in Trakl's poetry, mostly as a stillbirth; but sometimes
even stillbirth seems to refer to the first kind of birth, as will later be
demonstrated. The two possibilities are not, for Trakl, absolutely
contradictory, in the usual sense that death appears to be the anti-
thesis of life.

Moreover, the child's corpse at the end of "Offenbarung und Un-
tergang" cannot be exclusively associated with the poet, even though
it emerges from his shadow. We have already seen how the sister is

often identified with her brother. The poet calls the corpse a moon-like formation ("ein mondenes Gebilde"), and at the end of "Traum und Umnachtung" he refers to the sister as a moonlike countenance ("ein mondenes Antlitz"). At the end of the preceding paragraph of "Offenbarung und Untergang" he describes the sister as arising "auf mondenen Flügeln" (line 62). The sister is also associated with the moon elsewhere in Trakl's poetry, a point that Heidegger empha-sizes in his Trakl interpretation[27] (e.g., "Immer tönt der Schwester mondene Stimme / Durch die geistliche Nacht" in "Geistliche Däm-merung" [I: 118] and "Mönchin," a word referring to the sister and evoking a phonetically similar, hypothetical word, "Möndin," at the beginning of "Nachtergebung" [I: 164], echoed by "Mondeswolke" at the beginning of the third and last stanza of the same poem). But in an even more appropriate analogy to the end of "Offenbarung und Untergang," it is the dead sister who steps from the shadow of Sebas-tian, an alias of the poet, in a preliminary sketch for the poem "Sebastian im Traum."[28] The child's corpse at the end of "Offen-barung und Untergang" can therefore represent the sister as well as the brother.

The following untitled poem, first published in the critical edi-tion, contains two of the important motifs of the prose poems: the sameness of brother and sister (in the second line) and stillbirth (suggested in the last stanza).

> O das Wohnen in der Stille des dämmernden Gartens,
> Da die Augen der Schwester sich rund und dunkel im Bruder
>   aufgetan,
> Der Purpur ihrer zerbrochenen Münder
> In der Kühle des Abends hinschmolz.
> Herzzerreissende Stunde.
>
> September reifte die goldene Birne. Süsse von Weihrauch
> Und die Georgine brennt am alten Zaun
> Sag! wo waren wir, da wir auf schwarzem Kahn
> Im Abend vorüberzogen,
>
> Darüberzog der Kranich. Die frierenden Arme
> Hielten Schwarzes umschlungen, und innen rann Blut.
> Und feuchtes Blau um unsre Schläfen. Arm' Kindlein.
> Tief sinnt aus wissenden Augen ein dunkles Geschlecht.

[I: 314]

"Geschlecht" is another of the frequently used words in Trakl's poetry. It is used twice in "Passion" and it occurs even more often in the two prose poems. The word is ambivalent both in its meaning and in its emotional value. Its usual meaning is race or clan; but sometimes, especially in "Passion," where incest is a predominant theme, it evokes its other meaning: sex. It usually has a negative connotation, as in "das verfluchte Geschlecht" at the end of "Traum und Umnachtung"; but it can also have a positive one, as in "die Schönheit eines heimkehrenden Geschlechts" in "Offenbarung und Untergang." In the last line of the poem quoted above, the dark "Geschlecht" that ponders out of knowing eyes evokes both meanings—clan and sex—and the knowing eyes could be the eyes of the poor little child of the preceding line, who is evidently stillborn. Or, on the other hand, they could be the eyes of the brother and sister, which, as the second line of the poem indicates, are the same. Or is there really no difference at all between the incestuous pair and the dead child since the union of the sexes in brother and sister and the new birth are, in the final analysis, one and the same activity, which signifies for Trakl *both* death and life? Is this the untold message of the angel at the end of the *Brenner* "Passion"? Does his appearance indicate the achievement of the union of brother and sister?

2
Androgynous Man

O, die bittere Stunde des Untergangs,
Da wir ein steinernes Antlitz in schwarzen Wassern beschaun.
Aber strahlend heben die silbernen Lider die Liebenden:
Ein Geschlecht. Weihrauch strömt von rosigen Kissen
Und der süsse Gesang der Auferstandenen.

[I: 119]

These lines form the last stanza of the poem "Abendländisches Lied."
Since the preceding three stanzas present a compressed history of the
Western world ("Abendland"), progressing from prehistoric innocence
to the Christian Middle Ages,[29] the modern age would then be the one
of "Untergang"; and the "wir" of the second line would refer to the
entire present-day race of the West, just as it does previously in the
poem to our forefathers. But "wir" also points ahead to the lovers ("die
Liebenden") at the end of the next line, who call to mind the end of
"Passion" where the angel appears from the grave of the lovers. And in
the second line there is another occurrence of the reflection motif
which we have seen in "Passion." The history of the Western world has
passed over into the personal history of the lovers. It is their destiny to
become one sex ("*Ein* Geschlecht"). In this possibly literal borrowing
from Novalis, one must understand "Geschlecht" primarily as sex and
secondarily as race.[30] After "die Liebenden" Trakl inserts a colon, thus
associating them with the "*Ein* Geschlecht" which immediately fol-
lows. Also significant is the fact that here, for the only time in his
writings, Trakl emphasizes a word. This is important to note because it

is also the only time that he makes direct reference to the unisexual concept.

In a conversation between Carl Dallago and the poet recorded by Hans Limbach, there is a further indication of the importance of this concept for Trakl.[31] In the course of this conversation Trakl calls himself a Christian in a most exclusive sense. Dallago reminds Trakl of such non-Christian men of preeminence as Buddha and the Chinese philosophers. Countering with the remark that they also received their light from Christ, Trakl seems to startle Dallago, who has recourse to ancient Greece. Doesn't Trakl think that mankind has degenerated a good deal since the time of the Greeks? Never could mankind sink as much as it did after the appearance of Christ, retorts Trakl. Dallago injects as his last argument the name of Nietzsche, whom Trakl dismisses abruptly by referring to his insanity.[32] One wonders what it was about Christ that attracted the poet so much. Trakl seems to provide an answer to this question when, after a pause, he fixes Dallago with his eyes and says: "Es ist unerhört wie Christus mit jedem einfachen Wort die tiefsten Fragen der Menschheit löst! Kann man die Frage der Gemeinschaft zwischen Mann und Weib restloser lösen, als durch das Gebot: *Sie sollen Ein Fleisch sein?*"[33] According to Trakl, the problem of sex belongs to the deepest questions of mankind. The solution for him is a Christian solution, the intimate union of the sexes in one flesh. The conversation with Dallago took place in January 1914,[34] when Trakl had only recently completed both "Abendländisches Lied" and the first version of "Passion" (see note 5). Since Trakl's religious sentiments seem to be essentially related to his notion of androgyny, a discussion of Trakl's "Christianity" is in order.

The poet came from a mixed religious background. Having a Lutheran father and a Catholic mother, he was raised as a Protestant in highly Catholic surroundings. Later when he was under the patronage of Ludwig von Ficker and was a part of the *Brenner* circle (in which the above conversation took place), he consorted heavily with Catholics who tended to hold unorthodox views. Although his own religious views do not give the impression of orthodoxy, his claim to be a Christian should be taken at face value. This point is important because several critics take issue with Trakl's Christianity, among them one who, strangely enough, was not himself the adherent of an orthodox point of view: namely, Martin Heidegger.

Heidegger leads in the right direction when he writes the following:

> Ob Trakls Dichtung, inwieweit sie und in welchem Sinne sie christlich spricht, auf welche Art der Dichter "Christ" war, was hier und

überhaupt "christlich," "Christenheit," "Christentum," "Christlichkeit"
meint, dies alles schliesst wesentliche Fragen ein. Ihre Erörterung hängt
jedoch im Leeren, solange nicht der Ort des Gedichts bedachtsam aus-
gemacht ist. Überdies verlangt ihre Erörterung ein Nachdenken, für das
weder die Begriffe der metaphysischen noch diejenigen der kirchlichen
Theologie zureichen.[35]

Here the philosopher indicates that what the word "Christian" actually
means is not clear and that neither metaphysics nor orthodox theology
can give the final answer. Rather, in Trakl's case, it must depend on
what the philosopher calls "der Ort des Gedichts," which he estab-
lishes elsewhere in his article as "Abgeschiedenheit," a concept that
has to do with his notion of "Sein" and will be discussed later.

So far I am in full agreement with Heidegger. A discussion of any
particular religious sentiment of the poet is futile unless it includes an
attempt to determine what makes this sentiment possible in the first
place. But Heidegger then goes on to say that any judgment about
Trakl's Christianity must refer above all to Trakl's last two poems,
"Klage" and "Grodek," in which the poet calls out in desperation, not
for Christ, but for the sister. And why, Heidegger asks, does the poet in
"Klage" call eternity "die eisige Woge"? "Ist das christlich gedacht? Es
ist nicht einmal christliche Verzweiflung."[36] In the preceding quota-
tion Heidegger spoke as a philosopher and drew from his own
philosophical thought; however, now he appears to speak as a moraliz-
ing theologian and overlooks the fact that the sister herself had become
for Trakl a kind of Christ figure and that in great distress even orthodox
Christians have been known to call on the Blessed Mother rather than
Christ. In presuming to know exactly what "Christian" despair is, the
philosopher forgets that even Christ on the cross cried out to the Father
to ask why he had been forsaken.

The question of Trakl's Christianity might better be left to the theolo-
gians and orthodox religionists, at least one of whom, Alfred Focke, a
Jesuit priest, seems content to accept Trakl as a profoundly Christian-
oriented poet.[37] Whether or not one chooses to regard Trakl as a Chris-
tian in the strict sense, one must admit that there is a strong religious
trend in much of his poetry. This is exemplified not only by his many
references to God and Christ, but by the almost numinous aura with
which he surrounds his relationship to his sister, especially in his later
poetry.

In "Abendländisches Lied" the lovers arise as one sex only after
passing through the bitter hour of destruction ("die bittere Stunde
des Untergangs"). The risen lovers cannot be called "alive," at least
not in a biological sense. But the lovers also do not appear to have

completely transcended earthly life and entered a state resembling the Christian heaven. Indeed, all that can be said with certitude is that the lovers have undergone some kind of transformation which is basically sexual in nature and which is endowed with a ritualistic quality, suggested in the incense and the rosy cushions in the next-to-last line. (See "der rosige Engel" at the end of "Passion" and the usual optimistic connotation that the color rosy has for Trakl.) The situation at the end of this poem is therefore similar to the one at the end of "Passion" and at the end of the next-to-last paragraph of "Offenbarung und Untergang"; the same motif of the lovers' resur-rection is evoked. But here, the end of the transformative process is indicated in the terse wording "Ein Geschlecht."

The longing for the fulfillment of human destiny in a unisexual being is by no means restricted to modern times; indeed, it repre-sents one of the most ancient aspirations of the human race. Nor is this aspiration to be considered merely as a primitive or non-Christian tendency, superseded by the advent of Christianity and subsequently stamped as regression or depravity. In treating the sub-ject of androgyny in the Christian era,[38] the French scholar of primi-tive religions, Salomon Reinach, points out that the Church has always officially supported the dignity of the marital state and recog-nized as part of the purpose of marriage the fulfillment of the sexual desires of the partners which might otherwise manifest themselves in wanton promiscuity. But there has also been another tradition in the Church, the Gnostic, dating from its very beginnings but branded as heretical for its belief that the world, the flesh, and therefore sexual procreation are inherently evil. Many of the early doctors of the Church were influenced by this tradition, among them St. Augus-tine, who wrote in his *Civitas Dei* that it would be better if married couples could procreate without experiencing sexual pleasure dur-ing intercourse (Book XIV, Chapter 16). Another scholarly saint, Ori-gen, actually castrated himself to rid himself of his sexual desires. In an apocryphal gospel there is a report of a conversation between Christ and Salome. Trakl may have been acquainted with the words, since they are also cited in one of the few books known to have been in his possession: Otto Weininger's *Geschlecht und Charakter*.[39] Reinach writes:

> Salomé demande à Jesus jusqu'à quand régnera la mort. Il répond: *tant que les femmes enfanteront*. Le même Évangile lui faisait dire qu'il était venu détruire les oeuvres de la femme, à savoir la génération et la mort. "Mon règne arrivera," aurait-il dit encore à

Salomé, "quand vous foulerez aux pieds le vêtement de la pudeur, quand deux seront un, quand ce qui est extérieur sera semblable à ce qui est intérieur, et que le mâle uni a la femelle ne sera ni mâle ni femelle."[40]

Striking in this quotation is the proximity of the act of procreation to death, a proximity also indicated in the poems of Trakl already discussed. Important, too, is the fact that the inherent eschatological yearnings of Christianity are here presented under the guise of a unisexual race of the future, the ideal Trakl seeks in his own form of Christianity.

Androgyny as an eschatological goal also appears in the thoughts of a seventeenth-century female mystic from Amsterdam, Antoinette Bourignon. She looks forward to the time when man will procreate as he did in the beginning, without sexual union. In this way Adam begot his firstborn, who, she believes, was Jesus Christ. The resurrection of the dead will be a return to this original state.[41]

Reinach takes pains to emphasize the importance of the notion of unisexuality throughout the Christian era. He points out that it is not merely a kind of mystical aberration; even the positivist philosopher Auguste Comte paid it some homage. Comte envisioned the time when all women could reproduce as the Blessed Mother and thus, physically independent of men, could become their equals. He saw this, however, as the result not of a miraculous intervention but of the natural progress of science and evolution.[42]

Androgyny as the goal of mankind also enjoyed a certain vogue among the German Romanticists. Concerned with penetrating to a level of human experience they felt had been neglected by the men of the age of "Enlightenment" and the Olympian figures of German Classicism who had immediately preceded them, they harbored no merely morbid interest in forbidden realms; rather they wanted to allow a kind of human wholeness to emerge which the assiduously constructed balance of the Classical period did not afford. It is not surprising, then, that they hit upon the concept of androgyny in their speculations. Novalis makes reference to it in the poem at the beginning of the second part ("Die Erfüllung") of Heinrich von Ofterdingen. In anticipating the ultimate union of the hero with his beloved, the Blue Flower, Novalis writes:

Nicht einzeln mehr nur Heinrich und Mathilde
Vereinten Beide sich zu Einem Bilde.—
Ich hob mich nun gen Himmel neugebohren,

Vollendet war das irrdische Geschick
Im seligen Verklärungsaugenblick,[43]

Friedrich Schlegel's *Lucinde* contains an allusion to the same ideal in a much more earthy context. The author is engaged in giving his beloved a very frank appraisal of their sexual life. He describes his musings as a "dithyrambische Phantasie über die schönste Situation in der schönsten Welt":

> Eine unter allen [Situationen der Freude] ist die witzigste und die schönste: wenn wir die Rollen vertauschen und mit kindischer Lust wetteifern, wer den andern täuschender nachäffen kann, ob Dir da die schonende Heftigkeit des Mannes besser gelingt, oder mir die anziehende Hingebung des Weibes. Aber weisst du wohl, dass dieses süsse Spiel für mich noch ganz andere Reize hat als seine eigenen? Es ist auch nicht bloss die Wollust der Ermattung oder das Vorgefühl der Rache. Ich sehe hier eine wunderbare sinnreich bedeutende Allegorie auf die Vollendung des Männlichen und Weiblichen zur vollen ganzen Menschheit.[44]

The author shifts what started out as a playful bantering on an intimate topic onto a plane of esoteric, mystical speculation—an interesting example of the blending of the sublime and the profane common to the Romanticists and also, although devoid of the playful aspects, to Trakl.

Having discussed androgyny as an eschatological goal, let us now turn to cosmogonic androgyny. Many of the ancient cosmogonies picture the first man as a hermaphrodite existing in an ideal state and endowed with divine attributes. The loss of this state was felt to be a real deprivation, from which arose the imperfections of man's earthly existence, among them the necessity of sexual procreation and death. In addition to the biblical account of creation, there is a Jewish mystical tradition which claims that the first man, Adam Kadmon, was a hermaphrodite. This notion was introduced to Europe as part of the Kabbalist teachings and appears in the works of the German Protestant mystic Jakob Böhme, whose significance for the Romanticists, Novalis in particular, is well known.[45] It had probably also indirectly influenced Antoinette Bourignon, who lived about the same time as Böhme.

One of the oldest and perhaps best-known recorded cosmogonic myths in which androgynous man plays a central role is the one which Plato has the comic playwright Aristophanes relate in the *Symposium*. The discussion revolves around the origin and the nature of love; and Aristophanes' tale represents an older, more simplistic view. One might be tempted to discount this tale altogether as a kind of comic interlude, were it not for the fact that elements of it appear in other cosmogonic myths. Among these elements are the fall of man from a perfect state and the unfolding of history as an attempt to reattain that state.

According to *Poimandres,* a Greek manuscript dating probably from the first century A.D., which is itself based upon one of the oldest documents of the Persian religion,[46] the "Nous," the progenitor of all creatures, is both male and female. He (or It) gives birth to the first human who is a hermaphrodite like himself. This first man, himself also a god, loves his Father's (Nous') creation as well as his own form. When he descends to the earth, he sees his reflection in the waters; and both material creation ("physis") and the man-god become infatuated with the reflection. Thus the man-god becomes a prisoner of "physis" and loses part of his immortality.[47] In Böhme's account of the creation of the first man, Adam is drawn in a similar way from his heavenly home to the baser elements of the world and becomes their prisoner.[48]

A central feature in these accounts is the Narcissus motif. Narcissus, a demigod who was promised a long life if he would never look upon his own features, disobeyed this injunction and died, longing for his own reflection in the waters of a spring. In a variant related by Pausanias, Narcissus tried to console himself for the death of his twin sister, his exact counterpart, by looking at his own features in the spring to remind himself of his sister. We have seen strikingly similar occurrences of this particular form of the Narcissus motif in Trakl's "Passion" and "Abendländisches Lied." In these poems the reflection is also associated with a downfall. In all of the above instances where the reflection motif occurs, there seems to be as well an attempt to attain through the reflection something lacking. Trakl, probably without knowing the origin and history of this motif, uses it in a way which has much in common with the essential aspects of the ancient tradition.

The poet's strange attraction to water is known from his biography. Water seems to have represented a kind of protection for him; it shielded him from the harsh realities of the world into which he was born. In the account of Hans Limbach already cited, Trakl claimed to have known nothing of his surroundings, except for water, until he was twenty.[49] When he was about eight years old he walked fully clothed into a pond and continued until he was completely submerged, only his hat remaining on the surface of the water to indicate where he had disappeared.[50] Erich Neumann stresses the psychological abnormality evidenced by such behavior, even at such an early age, whether it be interpreted as a subconscious death wish or a desire to return to the motherly, female element.[51] Toward water, too, the figures of Trakl's poetry often incline their heads, as if to see their reflection. In a poem first published by Walther Killy in 1958, we find the following lines:

> . . . Geist der aus Bäumen tritt und bittrem Kraut
> Siehe deine Gestalt. O Rasendes! Liebe neigt sich zu Weiblichem,
> Bläulichen Wassern. Ruh und Reinheit!
>
> [I: 337]

Here the waters are clearly the female element ("Weibliches"). Characteristically, the spirit ("Geist") sees its own reflection in the feminine element, the complement of its own being. Trakl indicates that the spirit was in a state of frenzy ("O Rasendes"); but that after the fulfillment, the union with the feminine, a state of peace and purity exists ("Ruh und Reinheit").

The following lines from "Jahr" contain the same motif which shows the desire of the male for his female counterpart: "im Hasellaub wölbt sich ein purpurner Mund, / Männliches rot über schweigende Wasser geneigt" (I: 138). In the poem "Kleines Konzert," Narcissus is mentioned specifically, although in a much more obscure context. The final line reads: "Narziss im Endakkord von Flöten" (I: 42). This probably means that the poet experiences his reflection in the flute music of the "small concert," a synesthetic image of which there are numerous examples in Trakl's poetry.

Quite often, however, the reflection motif is also the harbinger of death. In an early poem, "Das Grauen," it is the face of the murderer Cain that the poet sees in the mirror.

> Aus eines Spiegels trügerischer Leere
> Hebt langsam sich, und wie ins Ungefähre
> Aus Graun und Finsternis ein Antlitz: Kain!
>
> Sehr leise rauscht die samtene Portiere,
> Durchs Fenster schaut der Mond gleichwie ins Leere,
> Da bin mit meinem Mörder ich allein.
>
> [I: 220]

In the poem "Die junge Magd" the servant girl sees a frightening image in the mirror, betokening her death which followed:

Silbern schaut ihr Bild im Spiegel
Fremd sie an im Zwielichtscheine
Und verdämmert fahl im Spiegel
Und ihr graut vor seiner Reine.

[I: 12]

These poems illustrate the other aspect of the Narcissus myth—the fear, still prevalent among primitive peoples, of the deathly qualities of one's own image. The aged Mörike gives expression to this same fear in his free-verse poem "Erinna an Sappho":

Als ich am Putztisch jetzo die Flechten löste,
Dann mit nardenduftendem Kamm vor der Stirn den Haar-
Schleier teilte,—seltsam betraf mich im Spiegel Blick in Blick.
Augen, sagt ich, ihr Augen, was wollt ihr?
Du, mein Geist, heute noch sicher behaust da drinne,
Lebendigen Sinnen traulich vermählt,
Wie mit fremdendem Ernst, lächelnd halb, ein Dämon,
Nickst du mich an, Tod weissagend![52]

For Trakl, as well as for Mörike, the reflection motif can indicate death. But for Trakl it can also indicate fulfillment in union with one's female half—the androgynous theme.

The myths concerning the first man cited above indicate with what awe androgynous man was looked upon by the ancients. Marie Delcourt points out that the hermaphrodite, although depicted as a person in some of the later ancient art, was really more of an idea for the ancients, a symbol of some of their highest aspirations.[53] Zeus, Dionysus, and even Aphrodite herself were sometimes depicted and even worshiped in certain localities as hermaphrodites.[54] It is not correct, according to Delcourt, to discount such cults as mere aberrations, although they frequently did give rise, especially in later antiquity, to what would now be considered abnormal excesses. On the basis of evidence from certain legends, Delcourt draws the conclusion that the hermaphrodite symbolizes man's aspiration for the attributes of divinity, among them eternal life.[55]

In Trakl's poetry as well, androgynous and numinous qualities appear together. For Trakl, the sister, who is often identified with the poet, embodies these qualities. If the poet refers to himself as "Schläfer," he calls the sister "Schläferin," as in the Brenner "Passion" (see also I: 137, 382, 458). If the poet appears as "Fremdling," then the sister is the "Fremdlingin" (I: 168, 455, 459). If the poet takes on ascetic characteristics ("Mönch," "Novize"), then he addresses the sister as "Mönchin" (I: 161, 164). In the poem "Das Herz" (I: 154), the word "Jünglingin" suggests the sister and calls to mind references to the sister as a dying young man ("sterbender Jüngling" [I: 150, 168]). The poem "Ruh und Schweigen" ends as follows: "Ein strahlender Jüngling / Erscheint die Schwester in Herbst und schwarzer Verwesung" (I: 113). Trakl's "Schwester" appears therefore as a hermaphroditic being, and in his later poetry she assumes an increasingly numinous quality. As already cited, she is a flaming demon in "Traum und Umnachtung" (I: 149). But she also appears in a more positive role, especially in the last poems—another argument against those critics who emphasize only the depressed mood of these poems to prove their point of the poet's increasing sense of despair. When destruction threatens the poet in the second poem entitled "Klage" (I: 166), it is the sister whom he calls upon with the poignant words: "Schwester stürmischer Schwermut / Sieh ein ängstlicher Kahn versinkt." Indeed the sister seems to be the only bright spot of an otherwise disconsolate universe, as in these lines from the first poem of the same title:

> Schwester, deine blauen Brauen
> Winken leise in der Nacht.
> Orgel seufzt und Hölle lacht
> Und es fasst das Herz ein Grauen;
> Möchte Stern und Engel schauen.
>
> [I: 163]

In "Grodek" she appears under a martial aspect; her shade wanders through the battlefield to greet the spirits of the dead heroes. Her appearance is framed by lines suggestive of anything but despair, especially in contrast to the often-quoted preceding line: "Alle Strassen münden in schwarze Verwesung."

> Unter goldnem Gezweig der Nacht und Sternen
> Es schwankt der Schwester Schatten durch den schweigenden Hain,
> Zu grüssen die Geister der Helden, die blutenden Häupter;
> Und leise tönen im Rohr die dunkeln Flöten des Herbstes.
>
> [I: 167]

It is therefore not without significance when Trakl gives the name Johanna to the sister in an untitled drama fragment (I: 455–459) and in a little-known poem entitled "An Johanna" (I: 330–331). The name is strongly suggestive of "Johanna, die Jungfrau von Orleans," the French maiden who dressed in men's clothing to help her country wage war on its adversaries.[56] Marie Delcourt does not overlook this clear case of transvestism in her book about the hermaphrodite.[57]

This chapter has attempted to establish a relationship between the androgynous theme in Trakl's poetry (namely, at the end of "Abendländisches Lied," in the reflection motif, and in the "sister" motif) and androgyny as it occurs in mythology and Christian eschatology. The next chapter will seek to illuminate the connection between incest and androgyny in Trakl's poetry on the basis of the studies of C. G. Jung.

3

The Role of Incest in the Genesis of Androgynous Man

Incest often plays a significant part in the cosmogonic myths where the semidivine beings of the beginning are all closely related. As in the joining of Heaven and Earth, their union produces the life which populates the world. Even the biblical account of creation entails the necessity of incest at the beginning of the race, since all human beings are descended from a single pair of parents, Adam and Eve. In a variant to the Persian legend of the androgynous first man there is a triple incest which had the purpose of giving legitimacy to the Persian practice of marriage among blood relatives.[58]

A very thorough study of the theme of incest in literature and legend is provided in a book published in 1912 by Otto Rank,[59] a disciple of Sigmund Freud. The author sees the frequent literary references to incest between brother and sister as deriving from the more basic incestuous type of relationship between children and their parents according to the Oedipus model.[60] Thus the entire incest theme represents a throwback to repressed infantile fantasies of the child with respect to the parent of the opposite sex. This repression can manifest itself at a later stage of the child's development in the form of abnormal attachment of the brother to the sister and vice versa. The normal person is able, in conventional sexual relationships, to effectively sublimate the complex resulting from a system of prohibitory social taboos and thus completely overcome the infantile stage. This sublimation occurs also in the activity of the artist or writer, always with the release of a tremendous amount of psychological energy which plays a major role in the creative process. Thus the frequent appearance of the incest theme in literature and legend can be explained as the outgrowth of the sublimation of infantile fantasies. The inability to deal with these fantasies in such a creative manner produces the neurotics who, in extreme cases, are rendered helpless and useless for any kind of normal activity.[61]

The idea that art arises from a sort of sickness or abnormality is completely in line with much of the aesthetic theory since Nietzsche and is particularly evident in the literary production of Thomas Mann. Such a theory is not at all adequate to explain the theme of incest in Trakl's work, however; here one requires the additional light shed upon the subject by the works of C. G. Jung.

In Jung's theory the concept of dominant infantile fantasies in need of sublimation in order to assure a normal life yields to the role played by certain archetypal patterns which are basic to the race as well as to the individual human being and which are not bound to any specific stage of development. Far from being infantile, they represent some of man's highest ideals and aspirations. One such archetypal pattern is incest: in particular, the incest between brother and sister. Jung's explanation runs as follows: The endogamous tendency (incest) is an expression of a basic instinct in man. It is a kind of "kinship libido" which holds the family together and gives a feeling of security, of belonging to a whole. Incest, in a broader sense, represents a desire for the union of a whole spectrum of qualities which are related and therefore should belong together but are actually of unlike nature.[62] As soon as primitive forms of social organization began to emerge, such as the tribe, the exogamous form of sexual relationship became more and more dominant. Bonds were cemented between families through marriage in order to prevent the dissolution of the newly formed social units. The more the natural endogamous tendency was suppressed by the progressive organization of society, the more it tended to express itself on a more exalted level; it was now considered as the prerogative of gods and kings. To quote from Jung:

> The endogamous tendency finds an outlet in the exalted sphere of the gods and in the higher world of the spirit. Here it shows itself to be an instinctive force of a spiritual nature; and, regarded in this light, the life of the spirit on the highest level is a return to the beginnings, so that man's development becomes a recapitulation of the stages that lead ultimately to the perfection of life in the spirit.[63]

As all the barriers to exogamous marriage disappeared and only the incest taboo remained, the endogamous tendency found expression in Christianity through the ideal of brotherly love and on the political level through the formation of nations. At the present level of human development these institutions are in the process of dissolution; and the endogamous tendency, which still remains a potent driving force, must now express itself in such frightening monstrosities as the totalitarian state and mass-man. The goal of this force is the integration of man, the production of a wholeness, a unity. According to Jung, we are presently witnessing a remarkable acceleration of the process toward this goal which cannot be slowed down and will take the form of depersonalization and ruthless collectivization unless man participates in it with his whole being, meaning *consciously*. For Jung, the only effective antidote to this depersonalization is, first of all, the psychological integration of the individual personality, the union of the male and female elements ("animus" and "anima") on the conscious level. But this is by no means the final step in Jung's estimation:

> The inner consolidation of the individual is not just the hardness of collective man on a higher plane, in the form of spiritual aloofness and inaccessibility: it emphatically includes our fellow man. . . . Everyone is now a stranger among strangers. Kinship libido—which could still engender a satisfying feeling of belonging together, as for instance in the early Christian communities—has long been deprived of its object. But, being an instinct, it is not to be satisfied by any mere substitute such as a creed, party, nation, or state. It wants the *human* connection. That is the core of the whole transference phenomenon, and it is impossible to argue it away, because relationship to the self is at once relationship to our fellow man, and no one can be related to the latter until he is related to himself.[64]

In accord with Jung's psychology, Heinrich Goldmann in his *Katabasis* stresses the integration of the personality as the goal of the incest act in Trakl's poetry;[65] and this narrow statement of the goal is perhaps the only inadequacy of an otherwise excellent and helpful Trakl interpretation from the Jungian standpoint. In adhering too closely to the Jungian method and terminology, Goldmann fails to take into account the broader implications which the psychologist himself draws in the above quotation and elsewhere. Only in this broader sense is it possible to appreciate the full significance of the words "*Ein Geschlecht*," for Trakl's term indicates not only the union of the male and female elements of the individual in one sex but further connotes the union of all men in one race.[66]

The alchemical studies of Jung elucidate the connection between incest and androgyny. According to Jung, the goal of alchemy was also the achievement of a kind of wholeness; the production of gold from baser metals was an aspect which enticed only the lesser minds, thereby giving alchemy its bad reputation. The greater minds, among them Paracelsus, concerned themselves with no less a task than unlocking the secrets of the universe and believed that somewhere in nature there was a substance or a force in which heaven and earth, the supernatural and the natural, met and were one. All their efforts were directed toward attaining this goal, symbolized by the philosophers' stone, the "quinta essentia," and particularly the hermaphrodite. In some symbolic representations of the alchemic process both incest and the hermaphrodite play leading roles. Incest was symbolic of the process itself, the mixing of certain chemicals, and the hermaphrodite of the end product which was never really attained. For Jung, the entire alchemic movement represents a great thrust of the unconscious level of man's psyche, a desire to unite the conscious with the unconscious, the "animus" with the "anima." One must keep in mind that Jung's unconscious, unlike its Freudian counterpart, transcends the level of empirical, individuated, spaciotemporal reality and thus enables man to participate in a region which can best be described as the divine life.

Two symbolic representations of the alchemic process analyzed by Jung are the "Visio Arislei" and a series of annotated pictures contained in the *Rosarium philosophorum* (1550).[67] In both of these works a *hieros gamos* takes place, a *conjunctio oppositorum* symbolized by the incestuous union of brother and sister. And in both works the development of the incest theme is remarkably similar to that in Trakl's poetry. In the "Visio Arislei" there is a king who rules over a completely unfruitful land where only like mated with like. In order to alleviate this condition, the king acts according to the advice of wise men to mate his son with his daughter, with the result that the son dies. The son's corpse is enclosed, together with the daughter and the wise men, in a glass house at the bottom of the sea where they all undergo intense heat and other forms of torture. In the *Rosarium* series of pictures a brother and sister pair is also present. The second of these drawings shows them fully clothed; in the third they have doffed their clothing; and the fourth shows them sitting naked in a bath. In the fifth image they are copulating under water. The sixth image shows not two bodies but only one with two heads, male and female, lying in a tomb. The bodies have become fused in death. The Latin inscription over the image reads "conceptio seu

putrefactio": in other words, the decay of the old life is the genera-
tion of the new. The points of contact thus far between Trakl's poetic
account of the incest act and the two alchemic versions are as fol-
lows: In all three cases the incest act results in death and the lovers
are joined in death. In the "Visio Arislei" they are imprisoned in a
glass house under the sea where they undergo torture. The reader
will recall the thorny chamber in "Passion" and the whitewashed
room of the last paragraph of "Offenbarung und Untergang." These
are the underground rooms in which the transformation of the lovers
takes place. In the "Visio Arislei" the lovers are imprisoned under
water, and in the *Rosarium* version they copulate under water. As
already demonstrated, water plays an important role in Trakl's
world, frequently as the instrument of reflection. Just as the lovers
are united in one body in the grave of the *Rosarium* version after
their incest under water, so too in "Abendländisches Lied" they are
joined as *"Ein Geschlecht"* after the bitter hour of destruction sig-
naled by the reflection in the black waters.

In both of the alchemic accounts a resurrection from the dead is
the goal of the process. In the "Visio Arislei" the king's son rises, as a
variant would have it, after he is given nourishment from the fruits
of a mysterious tree. In line 48 of "Passion" the boy himself becomes
a snowy tree as part of the transformation process. Figure 8 of the
Rosarium series depicts dew falling from clouds to cleanse the two-
headed body in the tomb. The German text under the image reads:
"Hie felt der Tauw von Himmel herab / Unnd wascht den schwarzen
leyb im grab ab."[68] This calls to mind the purification stage of the
incest theme in "Passion": "Da in dorniger Krammer / Das aussätzige
Antlitz von dir fiel" (lines 54–55). The falling of dew is another of
the motifs occurring in Trakl's poetry, and not always with the nega-
tive connotation that Heinz Wetzel supposes:[69] e.g., in "Die Heim-
kehr"—

> Unter dunklen Fichten
> Liebe, Hoffnung,
> Dass von feurigen Lidern
> Tau ins starre Gras tropft—
> Unaufhaltsam!

[I: 162]

Here the falling of dew follows the words of optimism: "Liebe, Hoff-
nung."

The tenth and final image of the *Rosarium* shows the hermaphro-
dite risen from the dead. In his psychological analysis of these al-

chemic drawings, Jung writes that the symbolic purpose of the incest
act is:

> . . . to re-create that royal pair which every human being has in his
> wholeness, i.e., that bisexual First Man who has "no need of anything
> but himself." Whenever this drive for wholeness appears, it begins by
> disguising itself under the symbolism of incest, for, unless he seeks it
> in himself, a man's nearest female counterpart is to be found in his
> mother, sister, or daughter.[70]

The purpose of the incest act in the alchemic writings and in Trakl's
poetry is therefore the same: the production of a unisexual being
who is both the offspring of the incestuous pair and the result of
their own fusion into one person, their own achievement of
wholeness.

By stressing the several points of contact between the alchemic
writings and Trakl's poetry, I do not wish to convey the impression
that Trakl may have been acquainted with these writings; this is
highly unlikely. The purpose of this comparison is to show that the
same psychological forces aiming at unity or wholeness which were
operative in the alchemists, inducing them to express themselves by
means of certain symbols, were also present in the creative impulses
of Trakl, who used similar symbols in his poetry.

Part II:
Death and Time

Ist's ein Affe, oder ist's ein Stier
Ein Wolf oder ander reissend Getier
Hei lustig geschnäbelt zur Nacht—
Bis zweie nur mehr eines macht!
Und eins ist der Tod!
(from Blaubart)

4

Death in Trakl's Works

In its consideration of incest and the hermaphrodite as symbols of unity Part I has already indicated the central role played by death. The passage through death was a necessary prelude to the achievement of unity. The next two chapters will deal specifically with death in Trakl's writings. We will now see that death itself is the area in which unity is attained.

Throughout the centuries most people who have called themselves Christians have not considered death as an end in itself. If certain periods, such as the late Middle Ages and the Baroque, seemed to devote a great deal of attention to death, especially in its gruesome aspects, it was always as a gateway to a more fulfilling existence than the all-too-threatened earthly existence of the time. Poets and artists who wished to remind themselves and others of the transitory nature of their lives painted lurid pictures of the end of all flesh, but always in view of the eternal happiness which awaited the just. The dichotomy of life and death always pointed toward a higher life which transcended both poles of the dichotomy. The lengthy dialogue between the plowman and Death in *Der Ackermann aus Böhmen* ends not with a victorious statement of Death, but with the judgment of God which puts both parties in their places and opens the way to a transcendence in which Death cannot share.

A new attitude toward death seems to have arisen with the advent of Romanticism. Previously the regions of death and the divine did not appear to be coextensive. The hegemony of God over death was undisputed; and, except in some aspects of mysticism, God's realm was considered as that of light, of absolute being—the exact opposite of the realm of death. But in the *Hymnen an die Nacht*, Novalis praises night and death as the only region in which the power of divine love can become manifest. The fifth hymn celebrates the coming of Christ into the ancient world as the ushering in of a new era of night and death. Novalis, then, does not portray death in its macabre aspects; it is no longer a mere transition to another life. As the region where the new revelation originates ("der Offenbarungen mächtiger Schoss"), it possesses great beauty. It is not so much the life beyond death which is desirable; death itself becomes the primary aspiration of the poet, the ultimate promise of fulfillment. This Romantic attitude is also an essential characteristic of Trakl's own treatment of death. And, as in the case of Novalis, Trakl's way to death is intimately linked to love, which, however, unlike Novalis' tender love for his deceased fiancée, is now the "dunkle Liebe eines wilden Geschlechts" ("Passion").

The following lines from Trakl's puppet play *Blaubart* (1910) are indicative of the poet's feelings in regard to love.

> Es öffnet zum Brautgemach die Tür!
> Sein Geheimnis ist Verwesung und Tod,
> Erblüht aus des Fleisches tiefster Not.
> . . . .
> Lust peitschen Hass, Verwesung und Tod
> Entsprungen dem Blute, gellend und rot
> Komm zitternde Braut!

[I: 444]

The play's hero is a sex murderer who kills his victims in fits of passion. The same theme is dealt with in an earlier fragmentary drama, *Don Juans Tod*, as well as in the untitled drama fragment of 1914. It appears also in some of the early poetry, as, for example, "Melusine" [I: 259]. In these cases passionate love in general foreshadows death; in the later poetry, however, death accompanies, specifically, incestuous love, as in the last line of the stanza from "Frühling der Seele" referring to the meeting of brother and sister in the clearing of the forest: "Gewaltiges Sterben und die singende Flamme im Herzen" (I: 141). Passion ("die singende Flamme") and death go together for Trakl, especially the forbidden passion of incest which seems to be at the root of all of Trakl's later allusions to love.

Both Trakl and Novalis indicate that love results in death.[1]

Novalis' deceased fiancée becomes an ideal leading him to desire death for himself. His own early death is seen as a fulfillment of this desire. Both poets seek a union with their beloved in death. Both see in death a kind of all-encompassing medium which not only sets an end to life in a negative manner but surpasses life in every respect and, as a more fulfilling state of being, is actually preferable to life. The conclusion seems reasonable, therefore, that Trakl belongs to a tradition which began with German Romanticism. A comparison of a poem by Trakl on the theme of death with poems by Novalis and two other twentieth-century Austrian poets will further illustrate this point.

"Allerseelen"

Die Männlein, Weiblein, traurige Gesellen,
Sie streuen heute Blumen blau und rot
Auf ihre Grüfte, die sich zag erhellen.
Sie tun wie arme Puppen vor dem Tod.

O! wie sie hier voll Angst und Demut scheinen,
Wie Schatten hinter schwarzen Büschen stehn.
Im Herbstwind klagt der Ungebornen Weinen,
Auch sieht man Lichter in der Irre gehn.

Das Seufzen Liebender haucht in Gezweigen
Und dort verwest die Mutter mit dem Kind.
Unwirklich scheinet der Lebendigen Reigen
Und wunderlich zerstreut im Abendwind.

Ihr Leben ist so wirr, voll trüber Plagen.
Erbarm' dich Gott der Frauen Höll' und Qual,
Und dieser hoffnungslosen Todesklagen.
Einsame wandeln still im Sternensaal.

[I: 34]

This poem by Trakl appeared in the edition *Gedichte* published in 1913. It does not exhibit to any great extent the surrealistic incongruities of his later, so-called Expressionist poetry. The poem very simply describes a visit to the cemetery on All Souls' Day (November 2). The "Lichter" of the last line of the second stanza are suggestive of the lights which are traditionally carried by mourners on this day. The living ("Männlein, Weiblein, traurige Gesellen") appear as poor puppets before the power of death. The perspective of the poem is that of the dead themselves; they look with pity on the suffering of the living: "Ihr Leben ist so wirr, voll trüber Plagen / Erbarm' dich Gott der Frauen Höll' und Qual." The situation is thus reversed. The living are supposed to mourn the dead on this day; but here it is actually the dead who mourn the living and pity their futile "Todesklagen." The skeletal dance of death becomes the dance of the living ("der Lebendigen Reigen") which seems unreal in the prevasive reality of death. The second line of the third stanza refers to the dead specifically as the decaying mother and child. The poet makes no inference that they exist somewhere beyond the decomposition of the grave. The only other line in this poem which refers exclusively to the dead is the last line: "Einsame wandeln still im Sternensaal."[2] Their peaceful existence is contrasted with the gloomy, futile activity of the living. It would be naive, however, to interpret this existence of the dead as transcendent, although the word "Sternensaal" leads one to think of heaven. The location throughout the poem is the graveyard and there is no reason to assume that it changes in the last line.

The following is a stanza from "Lied der Toten" by Novalis which also deals with a cemetery and was destined for the continuation of *Heinrich von Ofterdingen:*

> Könnten doch die Menschen wissen,
> Unsre künftigen Genossen,
> Dass bei allen ihren Freuden
> Wir geschäftig sind:
> Jauchzend würden sie verscheiden,
> Gern das bleiche Daseyn missen,—
> O! die Zeit ist bald verflossen
> Kommt Geliebte doch geschwind![3]

Like Trakl's "Allerseelen," this entire poem issues from the perspective of the dead. And again the dead do not belong to some transcendent realm where death has been overcome. They continue to take part in the activities of the living; they rejoice in death which they consider a more fortunate state than pale earthly existence ("das bleiche Daseyn"). They present no grim forebodings of destruction but rather are themselves the bearers of joy which they make possible for the living.

Closer to the atmosphere of Trakl's "Allerseelen" are the words of Death in Hofmannsthal's *Der Tor und der Tod.* Death appears to Claudio not as a fearsome skeleton but as a great god of the soul from the family of Dionysus and Venus:

> Wenn in der lauen Sommerabendfeier
> Durch goldne Luft ein Blatt herabgeschwebt,

Hat dich mein Wehen angeschauert,
Das traumhaft um die reifen Dinge webt;
Wenn Überschwellen der Gefühle
Mit warmer Flut die Seele zitternd füllte,
Wenn sich in plötzlichem Durchzucken
Das Ungeheure als verwandt enthüllte,
Und du, hingebend dich im grossen Reigen,
Die Welt empfingest als dein eigen:
In jeder wahrhaft grossen Stunde,
Die schauern deine Erdenform gemacht,
Hab ich dich angerührt im Seelengrunde
Mit heiliger, geheimnisvoller Macht.[4]

The same atmosphere permeates the fourteenth poem of the first cycle of Rilke's *Sonette an Orpheus,* written, of course, after Trakl's death:

Wir gehen um mit Blume, Weinblatt, Frucht.
Sie sprechen nicht die Sprache nur des Jahres.
Aus Dunkel steigt ein buntes Offenbares
und hat vielleicht den Glanz der Eifersucht

der Toten an sich, die die Erde stärken.
Was wissen wir von ihrem Teil an dem?
Es ist seit lange ihre Art, den Lehm
mit ihrem freien Marke zu durchmärken.

Nun fragt sich nur: tun sie es gern? . . .
Drängt diese Frucht, ein Werk von schweren Sklaven,
geballt zu uns empor, zu ihren Herrn?

Sind *sie* die Herrn, die bei den Wurzeln schlafen,
und gönnen uns aus ihren Überflüssen
dies Zwischending aus stummer Kraft und Küssen?[5]

The question posed in the last stanza is to be answered in the affirmative. The dead *are* the masters of life who grant the living all good things from their abundance. Life and death are not two separate states of existence but rather different manifestations of one reality, as Rilke states in a letter to his Polish translator:

Der Tod ist die uns abgekehrte, von uns unbeschienene Seite des Lebens: wir müssen versuchen, das grösseste Bewusstsein unseres Daseins zu leisten, das in beiden unabgegrenzten Bereichen zu Hause ist, aus beiden unerschöpflich genährt. . . . Die wahre Lebensgestalt reicht durch beide Gebiete, das Blut des grössesten Kreislaufs treibt durch beide: es gibt weder ein Diesseits noch Jenseits, sondern die grosse Einheit.[6]

Although Rilke stresses here the unity of life and death and states earlier in the letter that both life and death are affirmed in his Duineser Elegien,[7] there are many indications elsewhere in his work that he sees this unity only under hegemony of death, as in the last stanza of the poem quoted above. Important also is the fact that Rilke does not think of death in a merely negative sense as the termination of life. For him death exercises a benign influence on life in its entire duration.

Trakl's attitude toward death is rooted in this Romantic and Neoromantic tradition. Several critics have pointed to the influence of the Baroque tradition in his poetry.[8] To strengthen their argument they refer to the poet's childhood in Salzburg, a stronghold of Baroque Catholicism. But the treatment of death in Trakl's poetry goes beyond that of the Baroque. Death is not merely contrasted with life as its antithesis; it is not the means of escape to some higher form of existence. It suffuses life and forms a unity with life.

For Trakl, to an even greater degree than for Rilke, the unity occurs under the hegemony of death, which in contrast to Rilke's view is not always benign.[9] Nevertheless, Trakl's treatment of death as an enticing goal intermingled with life clearly places him in the tradition exemplified by the verses of the other poets quoted above. As in "Passion," almost all of Trakl's human figures seem to be dead and yet continue to act as though they were alive in some way. His is the poetry of the living dead.

Part I has established that the "Ein Geschlecht" at the end of "Abendländisches Lied" represents the offspring of incestuous lovers who are also associated with the appearance of the dead child at the end of "Offenbarung und Untergang." I will now try to show how the lovers signal the appearance of another figure, the boy Elis, in a way which has thus far escaped the notice of the critics.

The boy Elis is often considered as one of the few bright spots in Trakl's otherwise gloomy poetic world. One critic, Werner Meyknecht, even refers to him as the "Inbegriff irdisch-beseligter Existenzmöglichkeit."[10] Such an interpretation overlooks the fact that in the first of the two Elis poems, "An den Knaben Elis," Trakl writes of him as one who had died long ago: "O, wie lange bist, Elis, du verstorben" [I: 84]. Whereas this poem begins with the "Untergang" of Elis,[11] the poem quoted below entitled "Elis" begins more optimistically:

Vollkommen ist die Stille dieses goldenen Tags.
Unter alten Eichen
Erscheinst du, Elis, ein Ruhender mit runden Augen.

Ihre Bläue spiegelt den Schlummer der Liebenden.
An deinem Mund
Verstummten ihre rosigen Seufzer.

[I: 85]

In the light of "An den Knaben Elis," the word "Ruhender" of the third line takes on a rather negative significance, calling to mind the repose of the dead. The same word appears in neuter form near the beginning of "Passion" ("Ruhendes unter hohen Bäumen"—cf. "Unter alten Eichen" in "Elis") to designate the dead one mourned by Orpheus. In the second stanza the blue eyes of the dead child Elis mirror the slumber of the lovers, thus indicating a connection between Elis and the lovers. The last line refers to the "rosy sighs" of the lovers. The reader will recall that rosy was also the color used in conjunction with the appearance of the angel at the end of "Passion" and the "*Ein Geschlecht*" in "Abendländisches Lied." Both poems ended in indications of a resurrection or rebirth in a new being. It is possible that Elis in this poem represents the being born of the union of the lovers. This time, however, it would be a stillbirth.

The other occurrences of the name Elis in the various versions of the poem "Abendland" strengthen the impression of a close connection between Elis and the lovers. In the lines from the *Brenner* version of "Abendland" which follow, the lovers and Elis appear in close proximity:

Silbern weinet ein Krankes
Aussätziges am Weiher,
Wo vor Zeiten
Froh am Nachmittag Liebende geruht.

Oder es läuten die Schritte
Elis' durch den Hain,
Den hyazinthenen,
Wieder verhallend unter Eichen.
O des Knaben Gestalt
Geformt aus kristallnen Tränen
Und nächtigen Schatten.

[I: 404–405]

Here, as in the poem "Elis," we find a reference to resting lovers (cf. "Schlummer" and "geruht"). While the indication of the repose of

the dead is only faint here, there is an even more definite sign of the
lovers' death in the final version of "Abendland," in which the line
immediately prior to Elis' appearance reads "Hinüberstarben
Liebende" (I: 134). It seems quite reasonable that the union of dead
lovers should result in the birth of a dead child. The remainder of
this chapter will attempt to establish this point more concretely by a
further examination of "Abendland."

"Abendland"

The *Brenner* version of "Abendland" (I: 403–408) has a total of 137
lines divided into five numbered sections. Trakl reduced the final
version to three numbered sections containing a total of 48 lines, a
little more than one-third of its original length.[12] The *Brenner* ver-
sion of "Passion" had been similarly truncated in the process of
revision. Much of what is unclear or only cursorily touched upon in
the final version of the latter poem had received a fuller treatment in
the earlier version. The same can be said of "Abendland," although
an additional motif seems to have intruded in the final version. The
last version of "Abendland," which dates from between May 1 and
approximately June 3, 1914 (see II: 244), ends with lines which
would seem in retrospect to be a prophetic anticipation of the com-
ing war:

> Ihr sterbenden Völker!
> Bleiche Woge
> Zerschellend am Strande der Nacht,
> Fallende Sterne.
>
> [I: 140]

Both the *Brenner* version and the final version of the poem were
dedicated to Else Lasker-Schüler, whom the poet had met during his
visit to Berlin in March 1914.[13] The occasion of Trakl's visit to Berlin
was a sad one. Trakl's sister was married to an older man from
Berlin, Alfred Langen, and was pregnant with his child. Just prior to
her brother's visit, she had suffered a miscarriage and was near
death. It was during this Berlin sojourn that Trakl wrote the *Brenner*
version of "Abendland" (see II: 244).

In accordance with the guideline established in the examination of
"Passion," the question to be asked with regard to "Abendland" is:
What occurs in this poem? The answer: the birth of a child—a dead
child. In the final version of the poem there is little to indicate this.
Indeed, the title of the poem and its last four lines quoted above lead

one to think of it as containing a historical perspective similar to the one in "Abendländisches Lied"—a lament over the declining West. But as is usually the case in Trakl's poetry, the historical perspective can never be isolated from certain elements which, though objectivized and cryptic, are basically of an intensely personal nature. The final version of the poem begins with the lines:

> Mond, als träte ein Totes
> Aus blauer Höhle,
> Und es fallen der Blüten
> Viele über den Felsenpfad.

[I: 139]

At first glance, the imagery appears to be completely impenetrable. The word "Mond" is isolated syntactically as an exclamation without an exclamation point—a practice not uncommon in Trakl's poetry. Perhaps Trakl is employing a most extraordinary simile to describe the rising of the moon: as if something dead were emerging from a blue cave. The reader will recall, however, that "moon" and "moonlike" are sometimes used in connection with the sister and that the dead child emerging from the shadow of the poet at the end of "Offenbarung und Untergang" is called "ein mondenes Gebilde."

I will venture the interpretation that these lines are a cryptic reference to the birth of a dead child, the "Höhle" being the womb of its mother, the sister, from which it appears. The first two lines of the above quotation from "Abendland" are different in the *Brenner* version: "Wieder begegnet ein Totes/Im weissen Linnen" (I: 404). The white linen could be the swaddling clothes of an infant; but thus far, there has been no specific mention of a birth.

The following lines from the first section of the *Brenner* version, none of which are retained in the final version, will help us further:

> Und es tönen
> Die blauen Quellen im Dunkel,
> Dass ein Sanftes,
> Ein Kind geboren werde.

[I: 403]

This stanza referring to a birth contains imagery which allows only a positive interpretation. The preceding and following stanzas, however, present a different picture. The first stanza of the poem speaks of the laments of women ("die Klagen/Der Frauen" [I: 403]). The second stanza, the one immediately preceding the stanza quoted above, continues in the same vein.

Hinstirbt der Väter Geschlecht.
Es ist von Seufzern
Erfüllt der Abendwind,
Dem Geist der Wälder.

[I: 403]

The fifth and sixth stanzas refer to a dead one—the same child, it would seem, whose birth was mentioned in the third stanza.

Denn es ist die Nacht
Die Wohnung des Liebenden,
Ist sprachlos das blaue Antlitz,
Über ein Totes
Die Schläfe aufgetan;
Kristallener Anblick;

Dem folgt auf dunklen Pfaden
An Mauern hin
Ein Abgestorbenes nach.

[I: 404]

Again Trakl uses the recurring motif of the opening of the eyes (here incongruously "Die Schläfe") over something dead. And in a motif frequently associated with the dead child (see p. 71), the dead one seems to follow the lover ("dem [Liebenden]"), the one opening his eyes.

The view of the dead child presented to the lover is a "Kristallener Anblick." Goldmann, who includes crystal in his treatment of Trakl's colors, sees in it a generally positive significance: "Es steht für Geklärtes, für gewachsene, feste und dennoch zerbrechbare Form, für 'sublimatio,' geläuterte, reine Substanz."[14] In the already quoted stanza containing the appearance of Elis in this poem, the boy's figure is "Geformt aus kristallenen Tränen" (I: 405). Crystal can be the attribute of childhood in general ("Anschaut aus blauen Augen / Kristallne Kindheit" in "Die Heimkehr" [I: 162]) and more particularly the childhood of the boy who dwells within the poet in "Offenbarung und Untergang" ("Seufzend erhob sich eines Knaben Schatten in mir und sah mich strahlend aus kristallnen Augen an" [I: 169]).[15] If one adds to the above evidence the fact that Elis is indeed long dead (see "An den Knaben Elis"), the conclusion seems warrented that Elis is the dead one referred to variously in "Abendland."

The dead one appears again later in the poem. At the beginning of the fifth and last section are the following lines, omitted from the final version of the poem:

Wenn es auf der Strasse dunkelt
Und es begegnet in blauem Linnen
Ein lange Abgeschiedenes,

[I: 407]

The reader will recall that in the *Brenner* version there are also lines, changed in the final version, in which a dead one appears ("begegnet") in white linen (see p. 61). Another reference to the dead child occurs at the beginning of the later entirely omitted fourth section: "Ein Knabe mit zerbrochener Brust / Hinstirbt Gesang in der Nacht" (I: 406). Trakl uses the boy "mit zerbrochener Brust" as a metaphor for the dying song in the night. It is interesting to note that the boy who arises after the death of the poet in "Offenbarung und Untergang" carries the attribute "sanfter Gesang" (I: 170)—the same metaphorical association, therefore, in reverse.

Assuming that the dead child and Elis in "Abendland" are one and the same, let us now consider the question: Does the text indicate whose child it is? In the *Brenner* version, the second section, where the appearance of Elis occurs, begins with the following stanza:

Wenn es Nacht geworden ist
Erscheinen unsre Sterne am Himmel
Unter alten Olivenbäumen,
Oder an dunklen Zypressen hin
Wandern wir weisse Wege;
Schwerttragender Engel:
Mein Bruder.
Es schweigt der versteinerte Mund
Das dunkle Lied der Schmerzen.

[I: 404]

The poem passes here from the third person of the preceding section to the first person. Two figures wander together in the night. One calls the other "Mein Bruder." Who is speaking? A variant to these lines suggests the answer:

Wenn es Nacht geworden ist
Erscheint dein Stern am Himmel.
An schwarzer Mauer
Stehst du eine gebeugte Bettlerin
Und die Wunde in deiner Brust
Singt das dunkle Lied der Schmerzen
Meine Schwester.

[II: 248]

In the light of the latter quotation in which the brother (the poet) is
evidently the speaker, we must consider the former quotation as
spoken by the sister. The brother appears here as a sword-bearing
angel. This, together with the olive trees and the cypresses, again
brings to mind the biblical realm. The angel with the sword is sug-
gestive of the angel who stood guard at the gates of paradise after
Adam and Eve had been cast out (Genesis 3:24—cf. the different
function of the angel at the end of "Passion"). The angel reappears
later in definite connection with the sister in lines from section 5
also omitted from the final version:

> Rührt die kristallenen Wangen
> Eines Mädchens der Engel,
> Ihr blondes Haar,
> Beschwert von der Schwester Tränen.

[I: 407]

The girl and the sister are one and the same in these lines—another
example of Trakl's apparently arbitrary use of different designations
for the same person.

The brother and the sister emerge, therefore, as two of the chief
acting figures in "Abendland." By implication, they are the lovers
who rested happily by the pond where now only a sick and leprous
one remains (I: 404). The word "Oder" which introduces the appear-
ance of Elis immediately thereafter accentuates the contrast in mood
between the two stanzas. The sick and leprous one at the pond and
the boy Elis are not, therefore, two mutually exclusive alternatives;
but neither are they necessarily associated. Indeed, since many of
the images of this poem fit even less clearly into a coherent
framework than the most obscure images of "Passion," they preclude
the consecutive, line-by-line approach used in the analysis of the
latter poem. Significant from the point of view of this interpretation
is, primarily, the close proximity in the text of the words "Liebende"
and "Elis." On the other hand, this proximity would, of itself, be
insignificant in establishing a parental relationship between the lov-
ers and Elis, were it not for the following: (1) the same proximity in a
more decipherable context at the beginning of the poem "Elis;"
(2) the birth of a dead child alluded to elsewhere in "Abendland;"
(3) the emergence of the brother and sister as the lovers of this poem,
an association which invokes the theme of incest and its conse-
quences, notably the stillborn child, as in the last paragraph of "Of-
fenbarung und Untergang."

As has already been implied, the biography of the poet provides additional support for the above conclusions. In a footnote Ludwig von Ficker intimates that the much-quoted letter of November 1913, in which the poet speaks of the collapse of his world (I: 529–530), may have had something to do with his sister's tragedy.[16] Since this letter was written some five months before Margarethe's miscarriage, Ficker could be suggesting that Trakl had some reason for believing that all was not well in his sister's condition at that time. There is nothing in the existing correspondence to indicate this, but most of the correspondence between brother and sister has been lost through either the deliberate or indeliberate actions of their family.[17] It is also possible that Trakl somehow felt responsible for his sister's condition. Perhaps he even vicariously experienced fatherhood in the offspring of his sister and her husband. This would indeed help to explain the strangely interwoven motifs of "Abendland" (viz., the birth of the child, the dead one, the brother and sister, and the lovers).

Whatever the significance of Trakl's personal life for the poem "Abendland," stillbirth is a frequently occurring motif in his poetry, and many instances of it appear long before his sister's miscarriage.[18] One such earlier instance, in which both the mother and the unborn child appear doomed to an imminent death, is the third part of "Im Dorf":

> Ans Fenster schlagen Äste föhnentlaubt.
> Im Schoss der Bäurin wächst ein wildes Weh.
> Durch ihre Arme rieselt schwarzer Schnee;
> Goldäugige Eulen flattern um ihr Haupt.
>
> Die Mauern starren kahl und grauverdreckt
> Ins kühle Dunkel. Im Fieberbette friert
> Der schwangere Leib, den frech der Mond bestiert.
> Vor ihrer Kammer ist ein Hund verreckt.
>
> Drei Männer treten finster durch das Tor
> Mit Sensen, die im Feld zerbrochen sind.
> Durchs Fenster klirrt der rote Abendwind;
> Ein schwarzer Engel tritt daraus hervor.

[I: 64]

The dead dog, the men with scythes, the black angel who steps from the room—all these are images of death in the context of an ill-fated pregnancy. The first draft of the poem was written in March 1913 (see II, 118)—fully a year before Margarethe's miscarriage. The black snow that falls through the arms of the pregnant woman calls to mind the snow associated with the birth of the dead child at the end of "Offenbarung und Untergang." The snow image appears again in a similar context at the end of a poem entitled "Geburt":

> O, die Geburt des Menschen. Nächtlich rauscht
> Blaues Wasser im Felsengrund;
> Seufzend erblickt sein Bild der gefallene Engel,
>
> Erwacht ein Bleiches in dumpfer Stube.
> Zwei Monde
> Erglänzen die Augen der steinernen Greisin.
>
> Weh, der Gebärenden Schrei. Mit schwarzem Flügel
> Rührt die Knabenschläfe die Nacht,
> Schnee, der leise aus purpurner Wolke sinkt.
>
> [I: 115]

Snow here and in the preceding examples seems to signify the disso-lution of the body of the child—not the grim prospect of decay, but a kind of ethereal disintegration. In two poems first published by Walther Killy from the "Nachlass," one of which has already been quoted (see p. 31), the motif of stillbirth also occurs. The other poem, "Gericht," contains the following reference in a rather impenetrable context:

> Tote Geburt; auf grünem Grund
> Blauer Blumen Geheimnis und Stille.
> Wahnsinn öffnet den purpurnen Mund:
> Dies irae—Grab und Stille.
>
> [I: 316]

But even in such an obscure context one senses, along with the pessimistic imagery, some positive aspects of stillbirth. The mystery and silence of the blue flowers call to mind the blue flower of the poet Novalis—itself a symbol of death, but death as the highest form of fulfillment.

These other, more positive aspects of the stillbirth or dead child motif are also not lacking in "Abendland." After the appearance of Elis in the second section of the *Brenner* version, the following stanza concludes the section:

> Anders ahnt die Stirne Vollkommenes,
> Die kühle, kindliche,

Wenn über grünendem Hügel
Frühlingsgewitter ertönt.

[I: 405]

These lines and the preceding stanza contrast with the first three
stanzas of this section with their pessimistic imagery and the
reference to a dead one (i.e., "Wieder begegnet ein Totes / Im weissen
Linnen"). Elis is this dead one; but at the same time he is the hope for
transformation and fulfillment—a fulfillment in death (therefore:
"Anders ahnt. . . ."). His influence extends over the words of the
stanza in the next section referring to the sacrament of the Eucharist:

Schon reift dem Menschen das Korn,
Die heilige Rebe.
Und in steinernem Zimmer,
Im kühlen, ist bereitet das Mahl.
Auch ist dem Guten
Das Herz versöhnt in grüner Stille
Und Kühle hoher Bäume.
Speise teilt er mit sanften Händen aus.

[I: 405]

The ending of an earlier version of the poem "Elis" clearly estab-
lishes the association between Elis and the Eucharist. After the
words: "O! wie gerecht sind, Elis, alle deine Tage," the poem con-
tinues:

Ein heiterer Sinn
Wohnt in der Winzer dunklem Gesang,
Der blauen Stille des Ölbaums.
Bereitet fanden im Haus die Hungernden Brot und Wein.

[I: 372]

The hungering ones call to mind the lovers whose sobs were calmed
on Elis' mouth earlier in the same poem. They are the ones for whom
Elis signals the end of suffering and the advent of fulfillment. The
bread and wine echo the corn and holy vine of "Abendland." Trakl's
use of this motif is similar to Hölderlin's in his long poem "Brod und
Wein." In both poems the connection with a church ceremony is
missing; the surroundings are secular and even non-Christian, but
filled with a "religious" significance in the broader sense of that
word.

The next stanza of the third section of "Abendland" contains
another association between Elis and the dead child.

Vieles ist ein Wachendes
In der sternigen Nacht
Und schön die Bläue,
Schreitend ein Bleiches, Odmendes,
Ein Saitenspiel.

[I: 406]

The being referred to here in the neuter gender is walking
("Schreitend") in the starry night. When Elis makes his appearance
in the preceding section, it is his steps ("Schritte") which resound
through the grove. The being here is a pale one, a breathing one,
again one from the realm of the living dead. We have already seen
how Elis can be identified with the dead one who follows the poet on
his wanderings at the end of section 1 (see p. 62).

The dead child not only follows the poet but points the way for
him. His fate indicates the fate of the poet, the "Wanderer." In this
sense the dead child assumes the role of a *psychopomp*, a Hermes-
like figure in the form of a child[19]—the part of the poet which is
already dead but goes on existing in a different realm. The last stanza
of the *Brenner* version of "Abendland" reads:

In kindlicher Stille,
Im Korn, wo sprachlos ein Kreuz ragt,
Erscheint dem Schauenden
Seufzend sein Schatten und Hingang.

[I: 408]

The cross rising in the childlike stillness suggests a connection be-
tween the dead child and the cross, which is more definitely estab-
lished in a fragment of a poem first published in the critical edition.
"Ein Kreuz ragt Elis/Dein Leib auf dämmernden Pfaden" (I: 429).
Elis is both the sign of fulfillment and the sign of suffering and death
in the form of a child. He is the shadow of the poet which points the
way to the poet's own death ("Hingang"). This is perhaps what Else
Lasker-Schüler means by the first two lines of her poem "Georg
Trakl": "Seine Augen standen ganz fern./Er war als Knabe einmal
schon im Himmel."[20] To put it more precisely, not only *was* Trakl as
the boy Elis already in a different realm; but he *continues* to exist
there with that part of his being which is already "dead" to the
world.

The next chapter will further discuss the dead child motif in its
relationship to the poet and his treatment of time. Martin Heideg-

ger's perception of this configuration in his Trakl interpretation and his analysis of death and time in *Sein und Zeit* will provide an important perspective for considering the significance of Trakl's death theme.

5
Trakl and Heidegger

The image of the dead child following the poet, as in the *Brenner* version of "Abendland," occurs in several other poems. The following lines are taken from "Am Mönchsberg":

> Immer folgt dem Wandrer die dunkle Gestalt der Kühle
> Über knöchernen Steg, die hyazinthene Stimme des Knaben,
> Leise sagend die vergessene Legende des Walds,
>
> [I: 94]

In "Jahr" are these words: "goldene Wolke/Folgt dem Einsamen, der schwarze Schatten des Enkels" (I: 138); and the first stanza of "Vorhölle" ends with:

> Dem Schreitenden nachweht goldene Kühle,
> Dem Fremdling, vom Friedhof,
> Als folgte im Schatten ein zarter Leichnam.
>
> [I: 132]

The situation can be reversed, however; a dead figure can also follow the boy. This occurs in "Der Wanderer," the first draft of which is the same as that of "Am Mönchsberg." In the final version of the former are the words: "Folgt dem Knaben ein erstorbenes Antlitz" (I: 122). Thus it would seem, on the basis of this last piece of textual evidence, that a typically paradoxical statement of Heidegger's is at least in part justified. In referring to the lines from "Am Mönchsberg" quoted above, the philosopher writes: " 'Die dunkle Gestalt der Kühle' folgt dem Wanderer nicht nach. Sie geht ihm voraus, insofern die blaue Stimme des Knaben Vergessenes zurückholt und es *vor-sagt*."[21]

The dead boy is the subject of one of Trakl's poems entitled: "An einen Frühverstorbenen."

> Jener aber ging die steinernen Stufen des Mönchsbergs hinab,
> Ein blaues Lächeln im Antlitz und seltsam verpuppt
> In seine stillere Kindheit und starb;
>
> [I: 117]

The location "Mönchsberg" is the same as in the title of the previously cited poem in which the dead boy appears. The Mönchsberg, a landmark in Salzburg, was familiar to the poet from his childhood. According to "An einen Frühverstorbenen," the dead boy had been a playmate of the poet and remained, even in death, his companion and conversation partner.

Two earlier poems in which the death of a brother is mentioned indicate an even closer relationship between the dead boy and the poet. "Der Spaziergang" has the words: "Ein Bruder stirbt dir in verwunschnem Land/Und stählern schaun dich deine Augen an" (I: 44). The incongruity of the second verse diminishes when one considers the eyes as belonging both to the poet and to the dead brother, who is really the poet's double. Such an identification is already familiar from "Passion" and elsewhere. The following lines from "Psalm" refer to a possible double in connection with a dead brother: "Der Student, vielleicht ein Doppelgänger, schaut ihr [der Schwester] lange vom Fenster nach./Hinter ihm steht sein toter Bruder" (I: 55). The student would most likely be the double of the brother, but conceivably also of the sister.

At the end of the fourth section of "Helian" is a stanza which immediately calls to mind the dead boy motif:

> Lasset das Lied auch des Knaben gedenken,
> Seines Wahnsinns, und weisser Brauen und seines Hingangs,
> Des Verwesten, der bläulich die Augen aufschlägt.
> O wie traurig ist dieses Wiedersehn.
>
> [I: 72]

An earlier stanza of the same poem speaks of a "holy brother," also in the context of times past:

Zur Vesper verliert sich der Fremdling in schwarzer
   Novemberzerstörung,
Unter morschem Geäst, an Mauern voll Aussatz hin,
Wo vordem der heilige Bruder gegangen,
Versunken in das sanfte Saitenspiel seines Wahnsinns,

[I: 70]

When Lachmann associates the holy brother with Hölderlin because
of the reference to insanity ("seines Wahnsinns"), he overlooks the
same reference in the later stanza about the dead boy.[22] The dead
boy and the holy brother are really one and the same. The dead boy
is thus intimately related to the poet, or to his poetic masks (viz.,
"der Fremdling," "der Wanderer," and "der Einsame"). But he is
actually more than just the brother of the poet; he represents the past
of the poet, as in the words of "Offenbarung und Untergang": "Seuf-
zend erhob sich eines Knaben Schatten in mir und sah mich
strahlend aus kristallnen Augen an" (I: 169).

On the other hand, we have seen that the dead boy not only fol-
lows the poet but leads the way for him. He stands not only for the
poet's past—his childhood—but also for his future—his death and
possible transformation. Thus, Trakl's poetry manifests no really
distinct time levels, but rather a time-whole in which his figures live.
In order to lend additional credence to this conclusion, let us now
examine the place occupied by another of Trakl's major figures, the
unborn one.

Trakl brings the dead boy into relationship with the unborn in
"Stundenlied" (I: 80). The scene is again suggestive of a stillbirth
following the union of the lovers: "Purpurn zerbrach der Gesegneten
Mund. . . . Und aus verfallener Bläue tritt bisweilen ein Abgelebtes."
But the lines immediately preceding "Und" seem to identify the
dead one with the unborn one: "des Ungeborenen/Pfad an finsteren
Dörfern, einsamen Sommern hin." The same poem ends with a line
that calls to mind the boy who dies at an early age in "An einen
Frühverstorbenen": "Im dämmernden Garten Schritt und Stille des
verstorbenen Knaben." In "Kaspar Hauser Lied" Trakl equates the
unborn one with the historical Kaspar Hauser, who died as a young
man. The last line of this poem reads: "Silbern sank des Ungebornen
Haupt hin" (I: 95). But in a variant of this line, Trakl extended the
comparison even further: "Eines Ungebornen sank des Fremdlings
rotes Haupt hin" (II: 163). Here he equates the unborn one with the
"Fremdling," the designation most frequently associated with the
mature poet.

The circle is completely closed in the poem "Gesang des Abge-schiedenen," dedicated to Karl Borromaeus Heinrich, a religiously oriented writer friend of Trakl's in the *Brenner* circle who later entered a monastery in Einsiedeln, Switzerland. The word "Bruder" occurs in this poem and in the poem "Untergang" (I: 116), also dedicated to Heinrich with the words "seinem lieben Bruder Borromaeus Heinrich statt eines Briefs" (I: 465). It seems safe to assume that the word "Bruder" in these poems refers to Heinrich. But as we have seen in other poems, this word also designates the brother of the sister, and sometimes even the dead boy, as the poet's younger double. Both of these secondary connotations are probably present in the word "Bruder" as it appears in "Gesang des Abgeschiedenen." One is reminded especially of the brother from "Abendland"—the sister's companion in the wanderings. In "Gesang des Abgeschiedenen" these wanderings also come to an end under the sign of the Eucharist:

> Und es leuchtet ein Lämpchen, das Gute, in seinem Herzen
> Und der Frieden des Mahls; denn geheiligt ist Brot und Wein
> Von Gottes Händen, und es schaut aus nächtigen Augen
> Stille dich der Bruder an, dass er ruhe von dorniger Wanderschaft.
> O das Wohnen in der beseelten Bläue der Nacht.
>
> [I: 144]

The next stanza speaks further of this blessed existence now broadened in scope to include a sequence of generations from the shades of the old ones to the lonely offspring, the "Enkel":

> Liebend auch umfängt das Schweigen im Zimmer die Schatten der
>   Alten,
> Die purpurnen Martern, Klage eines grossen Geschlechts,
> Das fromm nun hingeht im einsamen Enkel.
>
> [I: 144]

Finally, in the last two stanzas the transforming aura of the dead ones encompasses the poet himself as the "patient one":

> Denn strahlender immer erwacht aus schwarzen Minuten des
>   Wahnsinns
> Der Duldende an versteinerter Schwelle
> Und es umfängt ihn gewaltig die kühle Bläue und die leuchtende
>   Neige des Herbstes,

Das stille Haus und die Sagen des Waldes,
Mass und Gesetz und die mondenen Pfade der Abgeschiedenen.

[I: 144]

The poem ends with the word from its title, now in the plural per-
haps because of the reference in the poem to the shades of the old
ones ("die Schatten der Alten"). They also belong to the realm of the
dead, which here exerts a beneficent influence on the living: the
"Enkel"[23] and the patient one. The same end to the wandering in
peace and reconciliation which the brother had experienced now
awaits the patient one.[24] The dead ones ("die Abgeschiedenen")
refer not only to the dead of the past, those who have completed the
"Wanderschaft," but also to the patient one and the "Enkel," who,
like most of Trakl's figures, partakes in the realm of the dead. (See
the motif of the dead one following the poet in "Jahr": "goldene
Wolke/Folgt dem Einsamen, der schwarze Schatten des Enkels" [I:
138].) Moreover, instead of "die mondenen Pfade der Abgeschiede-
nen," a variant of the end of the poem reads: "die mondenen Pfade
des Ungeborenen" (II: 263). The fact that Trakl has exchanged one
"Chiffre" for another is not only an indication of the completely
random interchangeability of these "Chiffren," as Killy argues, but
here most significantly of the sameness of "der Ungeborene" and
"der Abgeschiedene."[25] The words that have been exchanged say
really the same thing; death stands at the beginning as well as at the
end of life. The unborn one meets his fate not only as the boy who
dies at birth or while still young, but as the "Fremdling" and those
who have struggled through life to become "die Abgeschiedenen."
Considered in this way, the unborn one is a symbol of an all-
encompassing death which reaches not only through all stages of life
but back (and forward) into potential life as well.

Death is the common denominator of all the figures that wander
through Trakl's poetry. In death they are all one and not merely
successive stages of a chronological development. In the analysis of
the preceding chapter, we have identified the offspring of the lovers
as the dead child Elis, who is therefore similar to the "Ein Ge-
schlecht" discussed in Part I, but not as an escape to a future tran-
scendence. As a child, Elis points just as emphatically to the past
of the poet and, like the "Ein Geschlecht," to the beginning of man-
kind, to the legends of the androgynous first man.[26] It is really mis-
leading to speak of past and future with respect to Trakl's figures.

Trakl often uses images connected with wandering: the path, the
steps, the way, or the figures themselves as wanderers or followers,

all of which are suggestive of a linear development toward a specific goal. Nevertheless, the conclusion reached in Part I—that Trakl's "Ein Geschlecht" is the goal of the incestuous relationship between brother and sister—must now be qualified. The desire for wholeness or unity manifested by the goal of "Ein Geschlecht" is really part of a more encompassing desire indicated by the lack of temporal distinctions in the development of Trakl's human figures. This development has no end and therefore no beginning; or, stated differently, its end is its beginning. This development is therefore not linear but circular—a circle whose center is death. Trakl's oeuvre ends with a line that is indicative of a new beginning: "Die ungebornen Enkel" of the poem "Grodek." (I: 167). They are apparently the violent pain that nourishes the hot flame of the spirit in the preceding line: "Die heisse Flamme des Geistes nährt heute ein gewaltiger Schmerz." (I: 167). But are they actually the sign of hope for the future? Could they not also be the once possible progeny of the poem's slain heroes whose death now precludes any offspring? Trakl's last poem thus ends with the same ambiguity that characterizes his poetry throughout. The poem "Jahr," in which the seasons coincide roughly with the stages of human life, ends with the line: "Goldenes Auge des Anbeginns, dunkle Geduld des Endes" (I: 138). These are not two diametrically opposed poles, but rather the complements of one another. The beginning anticipates the end, but the end also recapitulates the beginning. In the phrase "Dunkle Stille der Kindheit" at the beginning of the poem, Trakl uses the same attribute, "dunkle," which marks the end of life to mark its first stage. Both are dark; both are shrouded in death.

The circular structure of existence comes to light more concretely in Trakl's earlier poetry. The young poet's admiration for Nietzsche has already been mentioned.[27] Several of the earlier poems from the collection of 1909 contain unmistakable reminders of Nietzsche's eternal return of the same. In the first of the "Drei Träume" are the lines:

> Wie Blätterfall, wie Sternenfall,
> So sah ich mich ewig kommen und gehn,

[I: 215]

The third of the "Drei Träume" contains the following lines:

> Ich sah die Götter stürzen zur Nacht,
> Die heiligsten Harfen ohnmächtig zerschellen,

Und aus Verwesung neu entfacht,
Ein neues Leben zum Tage schwellen.

Zum Tage schwellen und wieder vergehn,
Die ewig gleiche Tragödia,

[I: 216]

Another poem entitled "Einer Vorübergehenden" (I: 255) speaks of a passing girl who seems familiar to the poet, as if she were a beloved from a previous existence.[28] In a poem entitled significantly "Einklang," the last two stanzas are as follows:

Im hellen Spiegel der geklärten Fluten
Sehn wir die tote Zeit sich fremd beleben
Und unsre Leidenschaften im Verbluten,
Zu ferner'n Himmeln unsre Seelen heben.

Wir gehen durch die Tode neugestaltet
Zu tiefern Foltern ein und tiefern Wonnen,
Darin die unbekannte Gottheit waltet—
Und uns vollenden ewig neue Sonnen.

[I: 244]

As these poems show, Trakl apparently accepted Nietzsche's view of the circular structure of existence. In Trakl's later poetry, however, this structure is revealed not by repetition in successive existences but by the blending of beginning and end in the same existence. Here Martin Heidegger's interpretation of Trakl's poetry, in which the philosopher draws from his own concept of time, makes a significant contribution. In reference to the last line of "Jahr" Heidegger writes:

Das Ende ist hier nicht die Folge und das Verklingen des Anbeginns. Das Ende geht, nämlich als das Ende des verwesenden Geschlechtes, dem Anbeginn des ungeborenen Geschlechtes voraus. Der Anbeginn hat jedoch als die frühere Frühe das Ende schon überholt.
   Diese Frühe verwahrt das immer noch verhüllte ursprüngliche Wesen der Zeit. Es bleibt dem herrschenden Denken auch fernerhin verschlossen, solange die seit Aristoteles überall noch massgebende Vorstellung von der Zeit in Geltung bleibt. Danach ist die Zeit, mag man sie mechanisch oder dynamisch oder vom Atomzerfall her vorstellen, die Dimension der quantitativen oder qualitativen Berechnung der Dauer, die im Nacheinander abläuft.
   Aber die wahre Zeit ist Ankunft des Gewesenen. Dieses ist nicht das Vergangene, sondern die Versammlung des Wesenden, die aller

Ankunft voraufgeht, indem sie als solche Versammlung sich in ihr je Früheres zurückbirgt.[29]

This quotation, as difficult as it is to understand in itself, already indicates what Heidegger's concept of time entails: the linking of the future with the past ("Ankunft des Gewesenen"), which, according to Heidegger, is also how Trakl deals with time in his poetry. For Trakl, past and future are linked together in what Heidegger calls "Abgeschiedenheit," the "Ort des Gedichts." In the introduction to his essay on Trakl, Heidegger claims that every great poet writes from one single poem.[30] Although this poem remains unspoken, the interpretation ("das Denken") can, by examining the spoken words of the individual poems, ascertain the unifying idea ("der Ort") of these poems. By designating this idea as "Abgeschiedenheit," Heidegger not only alludes to Trakl's "Gesang des Abgeschiedenen" but also calls to mind an important concept of German mysticism from the writings of Meister Eckhart, with which Trakl was possibly also acquainted.[31] (Grimms' *Deutsches Wörterbuch*, in fact, lists the mystical significance of "Abgeschiedenheit" ["Abgescheidenheit" in the older spelling] in the first position, showing only a later development to the secularized usage as "Zurückgezogenheit," "Abgesondertheit," "Einsamkeit," "Entrücktheit" [Neubearbeitung, pp. 303–304]. The past participle and adjective "abgeschieden" reveals a similar original meaning and later development [p. 775].) In his tract entitled "Von Abegescheidenheit," Eckhart describes a virtue which is higher even than love and which consists in divesting the soul of every material thought and desire, thereby producing an emptiness, a kind of vacuum around the soul, forcing God to fill the soul with His own essence.[32]

This is not, however, what Heidegger means by "Abgeschiedenheit." Nor does he mean exclusively the realm of physical death, although the semantically sensitive philosopher undoubtedly wishes to evoke both of these connotations—the mystical and the concrete. "Abgeschiedenheit" is, primarily, the unifying principle which draws the past and the future, birth and death, into a whole. It transcends time and makes time possible, but not as something eternal or supernatural. It belongs to this world and directs all existence in the temporal order, and yet in the final analysis it remains a mystery since it has nothing to do with reality as one is accustomed to comprehend it. In this essay Heidegger's further explanations serve to point the way to an understanding of this concept, but they do not fully explain it. Like his concept of "Sein," the guiding light of his philosophy, the notion of "Abgeschiedenheit" is reached only approximately, and never by a direct statement. It has this ineffable quality in common with the mystical notion of Meister Eckhart.

> Diese [die Abgeschiedenheit] erschöpft sich nicht in einem blossen Zustand, dem des Verstorbenseins, worin der Knabe Elis lebt.
> Zur Abgeschiedenheit gehört die Frühe der stilleren Kindheit, gehört die blaue Nacht, gehören die nächtigen Pfade des Fremdlings, gehört der nächtliche Flügelschlag der Seele, gehört schon die Dämmerung als das Tor zum Untergang.
> Die Abgeschiedenheit versammelt dieses Zusammengehörende, aber nicht nachträglich, sondern so, dass sie sich in seine schon waltende Versammlung entfaltet.[33]

Existence appears as a unity when seen from the vantage point of "Abgeschiedenheit," which is not merely a condition, that of death, nor a concept formulated *a posteriori*. It draws into a whole all the stages of human existence symbolized by the various human figures of Trakl's poetry.

> Sie [die Abgeschiedenheit] ist erst dann der vollendete Ort des Gedichtes, wenn sie als Versammlung der stilleren Kindheit und als Grab des Fremdlings zugleich jene zu sich versammelt, die dem Frühverstorbenen in den Untergang folgen, indem sie, ihm nachlauschend, den Wohllaut seines Pfades in die Verlautbarung der gesprochenen Sprache bringen und so die Abgeschiedenen werden.[34]

There are other things in this essay with which one would have to take issue (see pp. 34–35). Heidegger is probably most vulnerable when he indulges in etymological investigation to demonstrate a point.[35] These dubious etymological excursions do not detract, however, from the major points that Heidegger makes in his essay: namely, first of all, that all great poetry, and in particular Trakl's poetry, originates from a single poem. Killy concurs in this conclusion, although from different premises.[36] Second, his concept of "Abgeschiedenheit" as the unifying center of Trakl's poetry is appropriate if one realizes that he means death in a nonphysical sense. It is a death which in some mysterious way informs all the acting figures as well as the landscape and the entire mood of Trakl's poetry. It is a death which stands not only at the end over the grave of the lovers but also at the beginning with the unborn one and the boy Elis; or, more exactly, it is a death which *nullifies* both end and beginning as valid concepts by creating a time-whole.

A major objection to this line of investigation still remains: its apparently fantastic nature, its alienation from what is considered real. Against this objection it might be argued that Trakl's poetry itself, as in the case of much of the writing referred to as "Expressionist," does not conform to reality. Therefore, if it is to be grasped at all conceptually, it must be by means of concepts which, themselves, do not depend on reality as we know it. Heidegger's *Sein und Zeit* provides such concepts which can aid in the interpretation of Trakl's poetry.

One should be aware that Heidegger also belongs to the so-called Expressionist generation. He was born just two years after Trakl in 1889 and wrote his doctoral dissertation in the year of Trakl's death. It is known that he became interested in Trakl early and read his poetry avidly,[37] although his first public acknowledgment of this interest did not occur until the early 1950s when he gave two lectures on Trakl near Baden-Baden. These were later published (I have quoted from one above). His *Sein und Zeit*, first published in 1927, could be considered a philosophical statement of Expressionism, at least in its approach to the problem of reality. Heidegger simply sweeps aside the centuries of philosophical bickering over the basis of this problem, the separation of the thinking subject from the contemplated object, by denying that such a split exists. For him there is no such thing as a subject here and an object there which somehow must be brought together *a posteriori* to verify reality. This denial is basic to Heidegger's philosophy and runs through all his writings. In this respect the gap between *Sein und Zeit* and the subsequent works is not as great as is often claimed. In *Sein und Zeit* he writes:

> Im Sichrichten auf . . . und Erfassen geht das Dasein nicht etwa erst aus seiner Innensphäre hinaus, in die es zunächst verkapselt ist, sondern es ist seiner primären Seinsart nach immer schon "draussen" bei einem begegnenden Seienden der je schon entdeckten Welt.[38]

Man is always "in the world" which has already opened itself to him. How is the world open ("entdeckt") to man? Heidegger answers: never primarily as "Vorhandenheit" (reality in the traditional sense), but as "Zuhandenheit":

> Sofern sich ihm überhaupt ein *Seiendes* zeigt, das heisst, sofern es in seinem Sein entdeckt ist, ist es je schon umweltlich Zuhandenes und gerade nicht "zunächst" nur erst vorhandener "Weltstoff."[39]

By rejecting the traditional concept of reality, Heidegger bridges the gap between subject and object. The world is always there *for* man ("zuhanden"); it is directed toward man ("verwiesen auf") and man is dependent on it ("angewiesen auf"). Man ("Dasein") and his surroundings are therefore, in a primary sense, one.

Trakl also refused to be impressed by his surroundings if they were not intimately a part of him and left nothing for him to do but bask detachedly in their beauty. In an undated letter to Irene Amtmann, in which he expresses his dissatisfaction with Salzburg and his desire to return to Vienna, Trakl writes:

> Man könnte mich vielleicht undankbar schelten, unter diesem wunderbaren reinen Himmel der Heimat so zu sprechen—aber man tut gut daran, sich gegen vollendete Schönheit zu wehren, davor einem nichts erübrigt als ein blödes Schauen. Nein, die Losung ist für unsereinen: Vorwärts zu Dir selber! [1: 551]

This quote becomes all the more significant if we compare it with the view of another great German lyricist—Goethe, the "Augenmensch." Goethe's way to himself was precisely through the external world and its natural beauty, which he never tired of gazing upon and assimilating poetically into his lyrical work. One has only to read the Dornburg poems of the almost octogenarian poet to gain some appreciation of the almost fanatical devotion to nature which filled even his last years with a buoyant optimism. Trakl, on the other hand, goes as far as to refuse even the solace that poetic creativity might bring. When asked in the course of his already cited conversation with Dallago if his poetic work did not give him some satisfaction, he answered: "Doch, aber man muss gegen diese Befriedigung misstrauisch sein."[40]

If Trakl can be called pessimistic both in his outlook on life and in his poetry, then this term can also apply—with reservation—to Heidegger's philosophy as expressed in *Sein und Zeit*, the second section of which begins with an analysis of death. Here one begins to gain a deeper realization of what the philosopher and the poet have in common. For Heidegger as for Trakl, death does not simply come at the end of life; it determines life from the very beginning:

> Das Ende steht dem Dasein bevor. Der Tod ist kein noch nicht Vorhandenes, nicht der auf ein Minimum reduzierte letzte Ausstand, sondern eher ein *Bevorstand*.[41]

With an apparently arbitrary play of words, Heidegger seeks to emphasize his point. He does not seem to use "bevorstehen" in its usual sense of "to impend," thus referring to the future, but in the very literal sense of the parts of the compound, "to stand before," thus referring to the past. For Heidegger, however, "bevorstehen" refers to both future *and* past. He intends both meanings, and the play of words here is therefore not arbitrary at all.

In this second section of *Sein und Zeit* Heidegger is concerned initially with arriving at what he calls "das eigentliche Sein des Daseins" which is synonymous with the wholeness ("Ganzheit") of existence.[42] To this wholeness belongs death, but not death as experienced when someone else's life comes to an end. Death so experienced is something actual and real ("vorhanden"), not the same as our own death. In our own lives death is always possible but never actual, since our experience stops with death. To be precise, therefore, death is something which, because it is a possibility, cannot be considered a real presence; but nevertheless, because it is a certain possibility, it reflects back on our existence with definitiveness. We exist in the proper sense (i.e., wholly) only when we, as existent beings (not simply "vorhanden"), take full cognizance of our own certain possibility and thus go forward ("vorlaufen") into death. In such a way our existence is "das Sein zum Tode."[43]

Heidegger's concept of death is fundamental to his *Sein und Zeit* and leads over to the articulation of a new concept of time which underlies the elusive formulation "Ankunft des Gewesenen" in his later Trakl lecture. Heidegger rejects as inadequate the Aristotelean notion that time is a succession of separate and distinct "nows." This notion makes the present "now" primary and thereby reduces time to something real ("vorhanden"). For Heidegger, time is not primarily real but "ecstatic": It is always beyond itself in such a way that the future, the essential time, gives rise to both the present and the past.[44] He argues that we experience time properly in accordance with our own existence which is characterized by the ever-present possibility into which it is thrown ("geworfen"): namely, death.[45] Possibility (future) is therefore the primary category for Heidegger, contrary to the usual reasoning of philosophers which makes necessity primary.[46] Madga King, in her interpretation of Heidegger, concludes that since time was to be the horizon of "Sein" in that part of *Sein und Zeit* which has never been published, then "Sein" itself must contain a negative element of primary significance corresponding to the element of "not yet," of possibility, in human existence.[47] There are several references in Heidegger's later works to this negative element in "Sein," which can even manifest itself as evil.[48] "Abgeschiedenheit" in Heidegger's essay on Trakl is similar to his concept of "Sein." Not only are they both related to time, but "Abgeschiedenheit," like "Sein," also contains a negative element. It is not the wholly optimistic concept that W. H. Rey maintains it is in his polemical article dealing with Heidegger's interpretation.[49] Although some of the points made by Heidegger do seem to warrant this conclusion, there are also several instances in which he clearly stresses the negative element in "Abgeschiedenheit." For example, when discussing the meaning of "Geist" in Trakl's poetry ("Die Abgeschiedenheit ist geistlich, vom Geist bestimmt"),[50] Heidegger writes:

> Der so verstandene Geist west in der Möglichkeit des Sanften und des Zerstörerischen. . . . Das Zerstörerische kommt aus dem Zügellosen, das sich im eigenen Aufruhr verzehrt und so das Bösartige betreibt.[51]

In order to understand the Trakl interpretation correctly, Professor Rey should have taken into consideration the fact that Heidegger's fundamental concepts belong to an area in which optimism and pessimism play no role, as the philosopher himself states with regard to the concept "Weltnacht" in "Wozu Dichter?": "Gleichwohl ist die Weltnacht als ein Geschick zu denken, das sich diesseits von Pessimismus und Optimismus ereignet."[52] The same applies to the contrast between good and evil; and in this sense Heidegger's philosophy is similar to that of Nietzsche:

> In der Abgeschiedenheit ist der Geist des Bösen weder vernichtet und verneint, noch losgelassen und bejaht. Das Böse ist verwandelt. Um solche "Verwandlung" zu bestehen, muss die Seele sich in das Grosse ihres Wesens wenden.[53]

For Heidegger as well as for Trakl, all things are gathered together in death. Not only do beginning and end merge to form one, but also all the stages in between. All the experiences of existence are assumed into the time-whole—the circle of death. We have noted in a previous chapter that the declining times of the day and the year (evening, night, fall, and winter) are the most commonly appearing periods of time in Trakl's poetry (see pp. 22–23). These periods are in keeping with its melancholy mood and its pervasive atmosphere of death. But on the other hand, one cannot deny the existence of other more optimistic elements in Trakl's poetry—images of reconciliation, peace, fulfillment, and resurrection which continue even into the last poems. Their seldom occurrence is no argument against

their significance, any more than the barrenness of a landscape di-
minishes the value of a small area within it where an outcropping of
precious stones has been found. One might say, quite to the contrary,
that the barren surroundings even enhance the aspect of the jewels,
making them all the more appreciated. Moreover, these more opti-
mistic images do not contrast directly with the central theme of
Trakl's poetry—death—but are somehow contained within this
theme, since they are often inextricably intertwined with the nega-
tive aspects of death (see esp. "Offenbarung und Untergang"). The
strictures of logic are of no consequence here. In Trakl's poetry, as in
Heidegger's philosophy, it is the as yet not actual future—death—
which determines human existence and makes it "unreal."[54] One-
sided categories such as pessimism and optimism cannot adequately
describe death so conceived. Under its sway are such interludes of
peace and harmony as the appearance of the boy Elis as well as the
raging passion of the incestuous lovers. From it arise both the still-
born child and the "Ein Geschlecht." It draws together the beginning
and end of existence in such a way that they are really interchange-
able.

Theodor Däubler has recorded a part of a conversation which he
had with Trakl in the spring of 1914. Däubler writes in his memoirs:

> Mein letzter Ausflug mit dem Dichter zarter Traurigkeit führte von
> Innsbruck, auf lenzlichem Weg, durch Dörfer nach Hall. Damals lern-
> ten wir uns eigentlich kennen; er sagte oft Kindern, die wir trafen,
> behutsame Worte, sonst sprach er ununterbrochen vom Tod. Als wir
> uns am Abend lassen mussten, war mir's, als hielte ich ein Fili-
> grangeschenk von Georg Trakl in der Hand: sanfte Silben spürte ich,
> sorgsam zueinandergeblumt, klar als Wortsinn einzig ihm und
> mir. . . . "Die Todesart ist gleichgültig: der Tod ist so furchtbar, weil
> ein Sturz, dass alles, was ihm vorausgehen oder folgen mag, gering-
> fügig bleibt. Wir fallen in ein Unfassbar-Schwarzes. Wie könnte das
> Sterben, die Sekunde zur Ewigkeit, kurz sein?"[55]

Death for Trakl is not the mere instant of the ending of life, nor is it,
on the other hand, simply the gateway to eternity. It takes prece-
dence over that which comes before it (life) and that which follows it
(eternity). The so-called "second to eternity" cannot, therefore, be
short.

Däubler goes on to ask Trakl: "Fasst uns darum bei abgründigen
Gesprächen, auf steilen Stellen, im Leben wie an hohen Orten,
Schwindel?" To this Trakl simply nodded his head in assent.[56] This
exchange helps us to see Trakl, in his attitude toward death, more

clearly as part of the Romantic and Neoromantic tradition. Again the words of Death to Claudio come to mind:

> In jeder wahrhaft grossen Stunde
> Die schauern deine Erdenform gemacht,
> Hab ich dich angerührt im Seelengrunde
> Mit heiliger, geheimnisvoller Macht.[57]

And if Novalis had hoped to find unity with his beloved in death, so Trakl, in a much more exaggerated and desperate way, sees in death a kind of unity which is the joining of those only imperfectly joined in the passion of life. Just before the end of his wildly orgiastic puppet play *Blaubart*, which culminates in the sexual murder of Blaubart's bride, Elisabeth, and the collapse of the murderer before the crucifix, Trakl has his hero allude to the ultimate purpose of his actions. His passion must rage: "Bis zweie nur mehr eines macht! / Und eins ist der Tod!" (I: 445).

Part III:
Trakl and the World of Unity

Soweit ich die viertausend Jahre Menschheit übersehe, gibt es zwei Typen neurologischer Reaktion. Gespalten an der Empfindlichkeit gegen das Verhältnis des Ganzen und der Teile, repräsentiert durch Irritabilität gegen den Begriff der Totalität. Primat des Ganzen, τό ἕν καὶ πᾶν, zufälliges Spiel der Formen, schmerzlich und zentripetal: Inder, Spekulative, Introvertierte, Expressionisten, und rühriges Absolut des Individuellen mit dem Begriff als Registratur: Kasuistiker, Aktivisten, ethisch und muskelbepackt; ich halte zu der Reihe der Totalen. . . . (Gottfried Benn, "Epilog und lyrisches Ich")

6
Good and Evil

Let us return to a point touched upon briefly near the end of Chapter 5: the union of good and evil in Trakl's poetry. Heidegger has indicated that Trakl brings good and evil together in "Abgeschiedenheit." The union of good and evil seems to reflect an attitude of Trakl's, basic to all his poetry, in which he was probably influenced by Dostoevski and Nietzsche.

The atmosphere of evil in Trakl's poetry attaches, in many instances, to the theme of incest. For example, the poem that ends: "Im Park erblicken zitternd sich Geschwister" is entitled "Traum des Bösen" (I: 29). In his last poems evil appears as the threatened destruction of mankind. In the earlier works it is frequently a wild, sexual passion which culminates in murder, as, for example, in the puppet play *Blaubart*.

This play ends rather astonishingly in Blaubart's twice-uttered cry: "Gott!" The stage directions state that prior to the second cry, Blaubart collapses in front of a crucifix. In the conversation with Dallago, Trakl referred to Tolstoy as "Pan, unter dem Kreuze zusammenbrechend."[1] With this comment Trakl indicated his deep appreciation of Russian literature and at the same time suggested what attracted him to this literature: namely the union of the Dionysian and the Christian realms. He was especially drawn to the works of Dostoevski, one of whose characters—Sonja, the benevolent prostitute from *Crime and Punishment*—appears in his poetry (see I: 104, 105).[2] Dostoevski's heroes often attain an understanding of the meaning of life through the suffering caused by their baseness. There is something of this awareness also in the conclusion of *Blaubart*. The cry "Gott!" does not merely indicate despair or blasphemy but the dawning of a religious yearning and a hope for redemption which also accounts for the earlier action of the old man in kneeling before Blaubart with the words: "Hab nie Herr einen gesehn in der Welt—/Der so wie Ihr von Gott gequält!" (I: 441). This scene may derive from a similar one in *The Brothers Karamazov* in which the aged Father Zossima kneels before Dmitri Karamazov as a token of reverence in anticipation of the latter's suffering (Book II, Chapter VI). The words of the old man in Trakl's play hold God in some way responsible not only for the suffering but also for the criminal actions of Blaubart. Such a God is also a God of evil, as indicated by Blaubart's invocation of "Gott-Satan" in a variant to a fragmentary scene of this play (II: 486). Blaubart, on the other hand, appears to have assumed some of the qualities of saintliness. In him good and evil are joined in a most intimate way.

Trakl forcefully expresses the same intimate union between good and evil in the poem "Der Heilige":

> Wenn in der Hölle selbstgeschaffener Leiden
> Grausam-unzüchtige Bilder ihn bedrängen
> —Kein Herz ward je von lasser Geilheit so
> Berückt wie seins, und so von Gott gequält
> Kein Herz—hebt er die abgezehrten Hände,
> Die unerlösten, betend auf zum Himmel.
> Doch formt nur qualvoll-ungestillte Lust
> Sein brünstig-fieberndes Gebet, des Glut
> Hinströmt durch mystische Unendlichkeiten.
> Und nicht so trunken tönt das Evoe
> Des Dionys, als wenn in tödlicher,
> Wutgeifernder Ekstase Erfüllung sich
> Erzwingt sein Qualschrei: Exaudi me, o Maria!

[I: 254]

This poem from the collection of 1909 was written probably in 1906 at the latest (see II: 366), before Trakl was twenty. It shows that he united the Dionysian and Christian realms at the very beginning of his artistic production. The same reference as in the later *Blaubart* to God's torment of man ("von Gott gequält") occurs here. From the hell of his masochistic suffering the "saint" lifts his hands to heaven in prayer. The more orgiastic ("trunken") the cry of Dionysus, the more it is also a prayer to Mary, the Mother of Christ. The last lines of the poem reveal, therefore, a conscious and complete intermingling of the two realms. All of this suggests a parallel to Nietzsche, the hero of the youthful Trakl:[3] Immediately after his lapse into insanity Nietzsche signed his short letters alternatively as "Der Gekreuzigte" and "Dionysos."[4] A similar alternation between "Dionysos" and "der Gekreuzigte" occurs in Trakl's collection of 1909. Following immediately upon the poem "Einklang" with its suggestion of the Nietzschean eternal return (see p. 77) in the last two stanzas is the poem "Crucifixus."

> Er ist der Gott, vor dem die Armen knien,
> Er ihrer Erdenqualen Schicksalsspiegel,
> Ein bleicher Gott, geschändet, angespien,
> Verendet auf der Mörderschande Hügel.
>
> Sie knien vor seines Fleisches Folternot,
> Dass ihre Demut sich mit ihm vermähle,
> Und seines letzten Blickes Nacht und Tod
> Ihr Herz im Eis der Todessehnsucht stähle—
>
> Dass öffne—irdenen Gebrests Symbol—
> Die Pforte zu der Armut Paradiesen
> Sein todesnächtiges Dornenkapitol,
> Das bleiche Engel und Verlorene grüssen.

[I: 245]

The clear reference in this poem to Christ, the God of the poor, contrasts with the "unknown divinity" of "Einklang." But Trakl never entirely separates the Christian element from the Dionysian, nor the good from the evil. In the drama fragment *Don Juans Tod*, probably written sometime between 1906 and 1908 (see II: 489), Catalinon describes the situation of Donna Anna's sexual murder paradoxically in the following terms: "Gib acht! Hier ist die Hölle— sagt' ich Hölle?/Vielleicht des Himmels Eingang auch. Wer weiss!" (I: 449). The redemptive qualities associated with Christianity must be broad enough to encompass even the orgiastic, blasphemous destroyers of life. The redemption does not depend upon the contrition of the evildoer; rather it attaches to the act of evil itself. This is the ultimate significance of the religious trend in Trakl's works.

"Verwandlung des Bösen"

In Trakl's later poetry the intermingling of good and evil is not easily recognizable. "Verwandlung des Bösen," written in the early fall of

1913, is the first of Trakl's three longer prose poems. The evil referred to here at the end of the first paragraph is, as usual, linked to sex:

> Die Stimmen des Rohrs, hadernder Männer im Rücken schaukelt jener auf rotem Kahn über frierende Herbstwasser, lebend in dunklen Sagen seines Geschlechts und die Augen steinern über Nächte und jungfräuliche Schrecken aufgetan. Böse. [I: 97]

The word "Geschlecht" in this passage has the double significance of race, or clan, and sex (cf. "Ein Geschlecht"); but here again the emphasis seems to be on the latter, especially in view of the reference to "virgin fears" following soon after.

Near the beginning of this paragraph two figures appear who traditionally serve opposite purposes—the shepherd and the hunter:

> Eine Glocke läutet und der Hirt führt eine Herde von schwarzen und roten Pferden ins Dorf. Unter dem Haselgebüsch weidet der grüne Jäger ein Wild aus. Seine Hände rauchen von Blut und der Schatten des Tiers seufzt im Laub über den Augen des Mannes, . . . [I: 97]

Trakl seems to contrast the shepherd, the protector of the herd, and the hunter whose hands are bloody from the animal he has just killed.[5] Later in the paragraph he mentions a place of murder ("ein Ort des Mordes"). Does this refer solely to the murder of the *animal* ("Wild")? The poem "An die Schwester" speaks of the sister as "Blaues Wild" (I: 57). The third paragraph of "Verwandlung des Bösen" refers to a dead one in the feminine gender: "Leise läutet im blauen Abend der Toten Gestalt. Grüne Blümchen umgaukeln sie und ihr Antlitz hat sie verlassen" (I: 98). "Erinnerung," the earlier fragmentary version of this prose poem, clearly establishes the identity of the dead one as the sister: "Stille begegnet in feuchter Bläue das schlummernde Antlitz der Schwester, vergraben in ihr scharlachfarbenes Haar" (I: 382). Thus "Verwandlung des Bösen" also brings together the themes of incest and sexual murder. The sentence immediately following the one in which the sister's countenance ("Antlitz") deserts her reads: "Oder es neigt sich verblichen über die kalte Stirne des Mörders im Dunkel des Hausflurs; Anbetung, purpurne Flamme der Wollust" (I: 98). The latter part of this quotation implies the union of religious sentiment ("Anbetung") with lust ("Wollust"). We can conclude, therefore, that the sister is the victim of an orgy of lust and murder with religious overtones.

Her murderer is the hunter who appears near the beginning of the prose poem.

This conclusion must be revised, however, when we examine a sentence in the second paragraph where the poet, apparently addressing himself, writes: "Du, ein blaues Tier, das leise zittert; du, der bleiche Priester, der es hinschlachtet am schwarzen Altar" (I: 97). The poet is both victim and priest, a mergence made possible by the fact that the poet and his sister are one and the same person. The killing of the victim takes place in the framework of religious ceremony—a ceremony that smacks of evil ("der bleiche Priester," "am schwarzen Altar"). If the priest here represents evil, then the victim ("ein blaues Tier") would represent the good, not only because of the traditional innocence of the victim, but also because of the usual significance of the color blue in Trakl's poetry.[6] Good and evil, therefore, are united in the same person, the poet.

The religious theme continues into the fourth paragraph with an allusion to the sin of Adam and Eve:

> Silberner Schritt im Schatten verkrüppelter Apfelbäumchen. Purpurn leuchtet die Frucht im schwarzen Geäst und im Gras häutet sich die Schlange. [I: 98]

The apple trees (here the plural), the purple fruit, and the snake— these are the things associated with the Garden of Paradise. Trakl thus brings the sin of sexual murder into relationship with the sin of the first parents, the result of which was also death.

Is there to be any release from this sin? The fifth and final paragraph of the poem reads as follows:

> Ein Toter besucht dich. Aus dem Herzen rinnt das selbstvergossene Blut und in schwarzer Braue nistet unsäglicher Augenblick; dunkle Begegnung. Du—ein purpurner Mond, da jener im grünen Schatten des Ölbaums erscheint. Dem folgt unvergängliche Nacht. [I: 98]

The dead one here immediately calls to mind the dead one of the third paragraph: the murder victim, the sister. Now in the masculine, however, "Ein Toter" also refers to the poet, who identifies himself with the victim in the second paragraph. The words "das selbstvergossene Blut" signify that the poet as both priest and victim has shed his own blood. The blood issuing from the heart and the dead one appearing in the shadow of the olive tree are suggestive of the death and resurrection of Christ. Thus the dead one applies to all three: the sister, the poet, and Christ. The sister and the poet had been the chief figures thus far in this drama of sexual murder, but now Christ's appearance seems to complicate the plot. In essence, however, we have here the same phenomenon observed in "Der Heilige" and elsewhere: the union of the Christian and Dionysian realms, the redemption of evil *as* evil. The last sentence of the above quotation precludes thinking of this redemption in terms of salvation in a traditionally conceived heaven. The title of this prose poem does indicate that evil undergoes some kind of change; but this change does not seem to alter its character as evil. Good does not take precedence over evil or defeat it; somehow it seems to join with evil in the poet to form a unity ("Du, ein blaues Tier, das leise zittert; du, der bleiche Priester, der es hinschlachtet am schwarzen Altar").

A short poem entitled "Die Sonne," also of Trakl's later period, reveals in more succinct terms the conjunction of good and evil. In the first stanza three of the figures from the beginning of "Verwandlung des Bösen" appear: the animal, the hunter, and the shepherd. Here they are all "beautiful": "Schön ist der Wald, das dunkle Tier, / Der Mensch; Jäger oder Hirt" (I: 134). As the destroyer of life, the hunter stands in a more negative relationship to the animal than the shepherd, the preserver of life. Trakl, however, not only affirms both aspects of humanity, but also sees nature in this twofold perspective. In the third stanza are the lines: "Wenn sich stille der Tag neigt, / Ist ein Gutes und Böses bereitet" (I: 134). At first glance the line "Ist ein Gutes und Böses bereitet" seems to be just another example of the dualism, the fundamentally contradictory structure of Trakl's poetry noted by several critics.[7] Reinhold Grimm reasons further however: "Aber in Wahrheit meint er [der Dualismus] ja kein Entweder-Oder, sondern ein Sowohl-Als auch: diese Welt ist böse, indem sie gut und gut indem sie böse ist."[8] Other critics besides Grimm have seen indications of a union of opposites in Trakl's poetry but have not pursued this aspect.[9] Even Grimm treats the union of good and evil in a peripheral manner and ignores the other manifestations of unity in Trakl's poetry. The trend toward unity is not a peripheral phenomenon in this poetry but, as I am attempting to demonstrate, lies at its very core.

7:
Trakl's "Symbolic" Style

The previous chapters have dealt with certain themes of Trakl's poetry as they relate to unity. However, this entire effort would be ill-conceived if it could only adduce content-related signs of unity, since Trakl's poems, like many in the modern era, do not always manifest a coherent, recognizable content. Accordingly, the present chapter will analyze certain structural elements involving vocabulary and syntax which are common even to the poems whose content does not lend itself to analysis. First it will be helpful to distinguish my own approach to Trakl's style from that of other critics.

In addition to the term "Chiffre," critics have employed the terms "metaphor" and "figure" to designate the essence of Trakl's poetic language. In spite of the difference in terminology, there are really no clear-cut distinctions in the critics' explanations of these concepts. Killy's "Chiffre" is a noun or attribute, the meaning of which can never be precisely determined since it does not fit into a frame of reference deriving from external reality. Trakl, according to Killy, borrowed certain images from the real world around him; but his aesthetic manipulation of these images was completely without reference to this world.[10] Clemens Heselhaus takes issue with the term "Chiffre," based in Killy's usage at least partially on the poet's relationship to reality, and suggests, instead, "metaphor" as a more appropriate designation. The concept of metaphor, according to Heselhaus, is not at all based on a relationship between the mind of the poet and reality. Trakl's metaphor belongs solely to the sphere of the mind and has nothing to do with either an acceptance or a rejection of external reality.[11] Rudolf D. Schier disagrees with both these concepts on the grounds that they have as their basis some form of relationship between the mind of the poet and external reality. Even the word "metaphor" in its generally accepted sense indicates a transfer from one level to another (i.e., from reality to the mind) and a one-to-one relationship between the levels. The term "figure," however, does not imply any such twofold basis for the image, but rather a mixture of many elements (e.g., borrowings from the Bible and the works of other poets), an indistinguishable conglomerate. But even Schier concludes that Trakl's poetic language derives essentially from the overcoming of the world in the mind of the poet.[12]

All of these critics have in common the fact that they see in Trakl's language a phenomenon without a clear basis in the real world. In the final analysis, they all use this real world as their point of departure but do not attempt to define what they mean by "reality." It is undoubtedly the world which is perceived by the senses and whose natural laws are manifest to the intellect—in short, the world of concrete, individuated objects. But precisely this notion of the "real" is being questioned more and more in recent times. If Trakl's language is incommensurate with reality as we have known it, could it not, in some way, be an expression of a reality which we are just beginning to understand? This reality is, as I will attempt to show, much like the one to which Goethe refers in his definition of symbolism, the point of departure for my own approach to Trakl's style.

In *Maximen und Reflexionen* Goethe defines symbolism as follows:

> Die Symbolik verwandelt die Erscheinung in Idee, die Idee in ein Bild, und so, dass die Idee im Bild immer unendlich wirksam und unerreichbar bleibt und, selbst in allen Sprachen ausgesprochen, doch unaussprechlich bliebe.[13]

Here Goethe uses the word "Idee" to indicate the highest norm which the artist could only approximately attain in his work. This use of the word "Idee" is related to another of Goethe's key words, "Natur." For Goethe, true art and nature are both informed by the same eternal laws: "Ich habe eine Vermutung, dass sie [die griechischen Künstler] nach eben den Gesetzen verfuhren, nach welchen die Natur verfährt und denen ich auf der Spur bin" (H.A., XI: 168).[14] And nature, like the "Idee" of the above definition, is the all-encompassing reality which can never be fully comprehended: "Natur! Wir sind von ihr umgeben und umschlungen— unvermögend aus ihr herauszutreten, und unvermögend tiefer in sie hineinzukommen" (H.A., XIII: 45).[15] In spite of the multitude of individual beings nature has created, her reality remains that of unity: "Jedes ihrer Werke hat ein eigenes Wesen, jede ihrer Erscheinungen den isoliertesten Begriff und doch macht alles eins aus" (H.A., XIII: 45). Nature is "das ewig Eine," as Goethe writes in the poem "Parabase" (H.A., I: 358). Natural science for Goethe has thus an essential characteristic in common with aesthetic production: Both are concerned with the one reality that transcends the multiplicity of appearances. In the phenomena of nature investigated by the scientist and in the various symbols employed by the artist of the Goethean stamp, there are indications of the universal essence.

There is one important difference, however, between symbolism in Goethe's sense and the use of the term "symbolism" as applied here to Trakl's poetry. Goethe always tended to see the manifestation of the universal essence in the concrete natural objects before him: "im Besondern." "Wer nun dieses Besondere lebendig fasst, erhält zugleich das Allgemeine mit, ohne es gewahr zu werden, oder erst spät" (H.A., XII: 471). This manifestation of the universal in the particular is at the root of Goethe's concept of the symbol. For him concrete reality always directed the wise and patient observer to the universal force acting within it.

Goethe uses the term "Gestalten" (forms) to designate the particular in nature. But in addition to the concrete "Gestalten," the visible entities, he also speaks of the "Gestalt" which determines the life pattern, the development of the living being. One can think of it as a blueprint which designates the capacities and limits of the organism for each successive stage of its development:

Also bestimmt die Gestalt die Lebensweise des Tieres,
Und die Weise, zu leben, sie wirkt auf alle Gestalten
Mächtig zurück.

[H.A., I: 202]

An important concomitant notion to that of "Gestalt" is "Grenze" or "Beschränkung" (limit). Only by means of the limits set to the development of the organism is perfection possible: "Denn nur also beschränkt war je das Vollkommene möglich" (H.A., I: 202).

Such is Goethe's notion of reality on the biological level: a clearly conceived "form" which fixes the limits of the visible forms representing the successive stages of organic development. According to the poem "Dämon" of *Urworte, Orphisch*, this "form," as the hard and fast law of the organism, is beyond the influence of the physical world. It is eternal. "Und keine Zeit und keine Macht zerstückelt / Geprägte Form die lebend sich entwickelt" (H.A., I: 359). Goethe's concept of the "Urpflanze" is also indicative of the reality beyond space and time. And yet Goethe considered his original model of the entire plant kingdom as a fact verifiable by experience.

Goethe's paradoxical adherence to a belief in nature as an all-encompassing, unfathomable unity that was at the same time available to the observer in concrete manifestations was apparently beyond the comprehension of even such minds as Schiller's. Our notions of the physical world have changed considerably since Goethe's time, however; and perhaps it is therefore not as difficult for modern man to make the connection between the particular and the universal as it was for Goethe's contemporaries. For example, the natural tendency to view individual objects as separate and distinct "pieces" of reality is no longer considered scientifically valid. We know now that all matter is ultimately reducible to energy which is not at all capable of individuation. The belief in clearly delineated, observable forms ("Gestalten") and behavior patterns for all natural objects is no longer a prerequisite of modern scientific investigation.[16] When the poet Rilke, therefore, speaks of "Weltinnenraum," the one space which permeates all beings, it cannot be for us as mysterious or mystical a concept as it might have been for previous generations.[17] At the beginning of the Eighth Duino Elegy Rilke distinguishes between the "eyes" of the animal and those of man. The animal's vision allows it to perceive what Rilke calls here "das Offene." Man, on the other hand, is forced from early childhood to see "Gestaltung," which blocks the vision toward "das Offene."[18] From this, one can deduce that "the open" must be free of "formation," besides being free of death as Rilke states.[19] Moreover, by emphasizing the word "ist" Rilke indicates that the region of the open is more significant than the customarily perceived reality of formation: "Was draussen *ist*, wir wissens aus des Tiers / Antlitz allein."[20]

Rilke's attitude toward "Gestalt" exemplifies the difference between Goethe's approach to unity and his own. In Goethe's view, man could attain unity *through* the concrete objects surrounding him. For Rilke, the open, the region of unity, is attainable only after the appearance of concrete formation has been unmasked. Symbolism in the Goethean sense could therefore seem inappropriate when applied to Rilke's poetry. Considered in another way, however, Rilke's poetry—specifically, his Eighth Elegy—might be even more fundamentally "symbolic" than Goethe's. Symbolism, according to Goethe's understanding of the term, points the way to the universal ("das Allgemeine"). Both he and Rilke strive for the universal in their poetry, but Rilke does it more directly by negating the individuation which stands in the way. A poetic style which frequently exhibits a breakdown of individuation can also be called "symbolic" in this more direct sense. Whereas an individual poetic image, according to the Goethean concept of symbolism, contains the essence of the universal, a poetry whose entire atmosphere is lacking in concreteness and individuation gives a more direct indication of a universal essence, providing that this poetry also shows other evidence of such an essence.

The ensuing analysis will attempt to demonstrate the breakdown of concreteness and individuation in Trakl's poetry. Trakl accomplishes in poetic style what Rilke suggests conceptually in his Eighth Elegy. What Trakl's poetry doesn't have, however, when compared to Rilke's, are definite references to the emerging unity. Whereas Rilke uses the terms "Weltinnenraum" and "das Offene" and expands upon them in his poetry, Trakl only once uses the term "Ein Geschlecht," tersely and without explanation. The present analysis must therefore be seen in the light of what has been determined in previous chapters. The unity which the breakdown of individuation presages reveals itself as the unity of "Ein Geschlecht," the unity of death, and the unity of good and evil.

In Trakl's earlier poetry, prior to the volume *Sebastian im Traum*, there are numerous examples of what might be called the blurring of contours; this is indicated in the verbs used: "rauschen," "schwirren," "schweben," "flimmern," "zerflimmern," "schwanken," "flattern," "zerflattern," "fliessen," "strömen," "kreisen," "schwinden," "gleiten," "entgleiten," "wehen," "verwehen," "tosen," "sausen," "fliehen," "huschen," "zerstreuen." These verbs are indicative of a kind of hectic, dissolving activity. The frequency of their occurrence alone is not as striking as their use as predicates of objects with which such activity is not normally associated.[21] The following examples will serve to illustrate:

Weide sanft im Äther schwebt,   [I: 281]
An Fenstern fliessen Pelagonienbeeten,   [I: 284]
Bazare kreisen . . .   [I: 293]
Rund saust das Korn, das Mäher nachmittags geschnitten.   [I: 28]

Die Äcker flimmern in einem fort   [I: 33]
Im Mittag strömen gelbe Felder.   [1: 42]
Baraken fliehen durch Gärtchen braun und wüst.   [1: 53]
Im Abendgarten kahle Bäume sausen.   [1:62]

The poems "Der Spaziergang" and "Heiterer Frühling" present a number of such examples. The following are from "Heiterer Frühling":

Ein Wiesenstreifen saust verweht und matt,   [I: 49]
Ein wächsern Antlitz fliesst durch Erlen hin.   [I: 49]
Der Wald strömt durch den Abend herb und fahl [I: 50]

"Der Spaziergang" has the following examples:

Ein Haus zerflimmert wunderlich und vag.   [I: 44]
Dann hebt ein Baum vor dir zu kreisen an.   [I: 44]
Ein Schober flieht durchs Grau vergilbt und schief.   [I: 44]

Even the poet himself can be drawn into the general dissolution of his landscape:

Und deine Stirne tost durchs sanfte Grün.   [I: 45]
Und manchmal schwebst du leicht und wunderbar.   [I: 44]

Modifiers suggestive of the blurring of contours, such as "wirr," "ungewiss," and "vag," also occur frequently:

Weinlaub wirr ins Blau gewunden,   [I: 27]

. . . und ungewiss und süss verdämmert
Wie heimgesucht der Raum.   [I: 256]

Die Pappeln glühn in ungewissen Reihn.   [I: 278]

Die Schwestern gehen still ins Haus,
Und ihre weissen Kleider schimmern
Bald ungewiss aus hellen Zimmern,
Und wirr erstirbt der Büsche Gebraus.   [I: 271]

Sometimes the poet describes the dissolution of reality in even more direct terms. In the following two examples only the vague contours of objects appear:

Ein Kind steht in Konturen weich und lind.   [I: 49]
Man sieht Konturen noch von anderen Dingen   [I: 277]

Sometimes forms ("Gestalten") dissolve into nothingness:

> Gestalten schwanken jammervoll ins Leere. [I: 283]
> Auch fliehn im Rauch Gestalten aufgelöst. [1: 49]

Sometimes, as if moving in the opposite direction, the contours of humans and landscapes extend into infinity:

> Die Haide war einsam und unermessen. [I: 272]
>
> Und Mönche tauchen aus den Kirchentoren
> Und schreiten im Unendlichen verloren. [1:276]
>
> Der dunkle Plan scheint ohne Massen, [I: 19]
>
> Leise fliesst im Grenzenlosen
> Dort das goldne Waldland hin. [I: 25]

All of the preceding examples are consonant with the unreality one is accustomed to posit as an essential characteristic of so-called Expressionist poetry and of modern poetry in general. The objects are borrowed from reality, of course; they are not fantastic creations of the poet's imagination, such as unicorns and enchanted castles. But because of their distinctive modifiers and predicates they enter into an unreal context. Alfred Lichtenstein achieved the same effect in his poem "Die Dämmerung": for example, in the line "Ein Kinderwagen schreit und Hunde fluchen."[22] Here verbs from the human realm are applied to objects and animals. One can adduce similar examples from Trakl's poetry in which the poet achieves an unreal effect by a random use of verbs suggesting human activity for objects.

> O wie sie die braune Stille stören,
> In der ein Acker sich verzückt, [I: 11]
>
> Bald scheint ein Dorf sich geisterhaft zu neigen. [I: 36]

But the examples from Trakl's poetry cited previously are not just illustrations of unreal situations. His poetry is filled with innumerable such situations achieved in various ways. Many of these are created, however, through the use of words that specifically suggest the blurring of contours. Because of the large number of these instances, it would be wrong to assume that they are merely the result of an artistic whim of the poet, who could have achieved the same unreal effect by using other words. In the first volume of his mature poetry, Gedichte (1913), Trakl seems to have deliberately chosen words which indicate a dissolution of solid, individuated objects.

In his later poetry, especially that of *Sebastian im Traum* and thereafter, the use of specific vocabulary suggestive of the dissolution of *objects* is not so common. The poet now seems intent on rendering his *human* figures, including himself, as indistinct as possible.

Throughout most of the collection of 1909 the presence of the poet is a dominant feature. The first person singular abounds. As in the first of the "Drei Träume", one often has the strong impression of being merely a witness to the personal ruminations of the poet about his dreamlike fantasies:

> Mich däucht, ich träumte von Blätterfall,
> Von weiten Wäldern und dunklen Seen,
> Von trauriger Worte Widerhall—
> Doch konnt' ich ihren Sinn nicht verstehn.
>
> Mich däucht, ich träumte von Sternenfall,
> Von blasser Augen weinendem Flehn,
> Von eines Lächelns Widerhall—
> Doch konnt' ich seinen Sinn nicht verstehn.
>
> Wie Blätterfall, wie Sternenfall,
> So sah ich mich ewig kommen und gehn,
> Eines Traumes unsterblicher Widerhall—
> Doch konnt' ich seinen Sinn nicht verstehn.

[I: 215]

A number of Trakl's early letters justify the characterization of his art as preoccupied with the self and without bearing on the outside world. Writing to his sister Hermine in October 1908, Trakl depicts a nightmare of reality—a terrifying realization that senseless animal instincts are the basis of all human activity. He goes on more confidently:

> Vorbei! Heute ist diese Vision der Wirklichkeit wieder in Nichts versunken, ferne sind mir die Dinge, ferner noch ihre Stimme und ich lausche, ganz beseeltes Ohr, wieder auf die Melodien, die in mir sind, und mein beschwingtes Auge träumt wieder seine Bilder, die schöner sind als alle Wirklichkeit! Ich bin bei mir, bin meine Welt! Meine ganze, schöne Welt, voll unendlichen Wohllauts. [I: 472]

In such states of near ecstasy the exigencies of the outside world cease to be of any importance to the poet. His own beautiful world of infinite harmony arises within him, and from this world stems his poetic creation. His poetry owes nothing to reality and reflects only the dreamlike images of his melancholic euphoria ("Ich bin immer traurig, wenn ich glücklich bin!" [I: 473].

The letter to Hermine and a letter to another sister, Maria, were written shortly after the poet's arrival in Vienna for the start of his pharmaceutical studies. The letter to Maria, especially, shows his dissatisfaction with Vienna and his pleasant reminiscences of Salzburg. In an already cited letter which the poet wrote from Salzburg to Irene Amtmann in Vienna (see p. 81), the sentiment is just the opposite: The poet yearns for Vienna in his dissatisfaction with Salzburg. Here it is not the frightening animal world of senseless activity which the poet rejects, but the quiet beauty of his homeland. Both worlds are reality; both are not really part of the poet, nor do they play any significant role in his poetry. His motto is "Vorwärts zu Dir selber!" (I: 551)—a most uncompromising goal.

Soon, however, Trakl seems to have revised his intensely subjective approach to his art. In an already cited letter to Buschbeck written in late 1911, he speaks favorably of a revised poem in which he suppressed the personal element: "Es ist umso viel besser als das ursprüngliche als es nun unpersönlich ist," (I: 485). He now no longer seems to be occupied with the easy and harmonious flow of images of his own inner world but with something separate from himself—something he calls "truth":

> Du magst mir glauben, dass es mir nicht leicht fällt und niemals leicht fallen wird, mich bedingungslos dem Darzustellenden unterzuordnen und ich werde mich immer und immer wieder berichtigen müssen, um der Wahrheit zu geben, was der Wahrheit ist. [I: 486]

This cannot mean that Trakl now intends to advert to reality and make his poetry conform to it. His later poetry is even farther removed from the real world than his earlier works. The "truth," therefore, cannot mean the truth of the real world. Nevertheless, to the "truth" in Trakl's sense must belong, in some way, the suppression of the personality of the poet. Neither the outside world nor the inner world of the imagination are synonymous with the "truth." In this way Trakl seems to be moving toward the avoidance of the subject-object split which Heidegger seeks to overcome in his philosophy.

In an article Ingrid Strohschneider-Kohrs distinguishes between the ego manifestations in the poetry of other Expressionists and Trakl's use of the word "ich" in "Die Nacht," a later poem which begins with the line: "Dich sing ich wilde Zerklüftung" (I: 160).

> Dies *Ich* ist überpersönliche, sogar person-fremde Sprache, die . . .
> den Gesang selbst als eigenes Geschehen ins Wort hebt. Es ist ein sehr
> anderes *Ich*, das hier im Wort ersteht, als das in der grenzenlosen
> Hingabe an die Welt sich selbst wiedererkennende Ich der expres-
> sionistischen Lyrik, die das Bewusstsein einer Verwandlung des Ichs
> in die Dinge, einer Verwandlung der Welt in das Ich aufrecht erhält
> und ausspricht—wie bei Stadler: "Ich bin nur Flamme, Durst, Schrei,
> und Brand" oder bei Werfel: "Ich will den Tod der ganzen Welt
> umschliessen."[23]

Trakl's suppression of his personality in his later poetry and the
often intense torrents of laconic images help to create a kind of
objectivity. Interpretations which see in Trakl's poetry merely an
aesthetic experiment with language are therefore missing the mark
according to Strohschneider-Kohrs:

> In der Entwicklung der lyrischen Sprache während der letzten Jahr-
> zehnte zeigt Trakls Gedicht eine Eigenart, die ebenso weit entfernt ist
> von jeder Art intellektuellen Experiments mit der Sprache—wie von
> der Lyrik der nur inspirativen Ergriffenheit und der Sprachmagie.[24]

In Trakl's later poetry the frequent impersonalization of human
figures through the nominal use of indefinite neuter singular adjec-
tives is indicative of an imprecise objectivity and thus also of the
blurring of contours. Examples of this impersonalization can already
be found in the poetry of the volume *Gedichte*:

> Und Ungebornes pflegt der eignen Ruh.   [I: 50]

> Wieder kehrt die Nacht und klagt ein Sterbliches
> Und es leidet ein anderes mit.   [[I: 40]

The latter two lines could be an oblique reference to the intimate
relationship between brother and sister. The first two lines of this
poem ("In ein altes Stammbuch") read:

> Immer wieder kehrst du Melancholie,
> O Sanftmut der einsamen Seele.   [I: 40]

Originally the poet wrote "Schwester" instead of "Sanftmut" (II: 88).
In most cases, however, it is impossible to determine who is meant
by the adjectival nouns used.

> Geruhiges vor einer Schenke spielt,   [I: 41]
> Resedenduft, der Weibliches umspült.   [I: 41]

... Ein Dunkles zeigt im Schreiten
Sich oft an Mauern, die im Herbste stehn,   [I: 61]

Für Einsames ist eine Schenke da;   [I: 61]
Verwestes gleitend durch die morsche Stube;   [I: 58]

In the volume *Sebastian im Traum* the examples become more frequent: "ein Abgelebtes" (I: 80); "ein Träumendes," "ein Menschliches" (I: 87); "Ruhendes," "ein Goldnes," "ein Totes" (I: 125); "Männliches" (I: 138); "ein Krankes" (I: 139); "ein Fremdes" (I: 141). "Ein Dunkles" and "ein Totes" or other adjectival nouns designating the dead occur frequently throughout Trakl's poetry. It is appropriate that in darkness and death the impersonalization is particularly marked. In these areas individuation ceases to be in effect, and all things blend into one.[25]

The process of impersonalization includes the poet as well. Although the last of the prose poems, "Offenbarung und Untergang," is written in the first person, the reader does not have the impression that the narrator is a real human being. At the beginning of the third section the poet again uses an indefinite neuter singular—this time in referring to himself: "Am Saum des Waldes will ich ein Schweigendes gehn" (I: 169). In other poems he shows a definite tendency toward self-destruction—an intensification of the feelings indicated by the impersonalization elsewhere:

Fiebernd sass er auf der eisigen Stiege, rasend gen Gott, dass er
    stürbe.   [I: 148]

Dass endlich zerbräche das kühle Haupt!   [I: 125]

Thus far we have seen the tendency toward the blurring of contours in verbs, modifiers, and substantives. It is a process in which both inanimate and animate objects, including human figures, take part. The scope of this survey can be expanded to show another way in which the poet achieves the same effect—namely, through the random juxtaposition of images, a feature of style common to much of Expressionist poetry and, in itself, an indication of the lack of sharp divisions between the images. The title alone of one such poem by Trakl containing a loose string of images is an illustration of the blurring of contours. This title, "Drei Blicke in einen Opal," introduces a kind of triptych in which Christian and Dionysian colors are mixed against a somber background of death and decay. Just as the iridescent colors of an opal seem to blend together in an indistinguishable mass, so the various elements of this poem seem to merge inseparably. The following stanza is from the first section of the poem:

> Aus Schwarzem bläst der Föhn. Mit Satyrn im Verein
> Sind schlanke Weiblein; Mönche der Wollust bleiche Priester,
> Ihr Wahnsinn schmückt mit Lilien sich schön and düster
> Und hebt die Hände auf zu Gottes goldenem Schrein.
>
> [I: 66]

The first stanza of the third section is as follows:

> Die Blinden streuen in eiternde Wunden Weiherauch.
> Rotgoldene Gewänder; Fackeln; Psalmensingen;
> Und Mädchen, die wie Gift den Leib des Herrn umschlingen.
> Gestalten schreiten wächsernstarr durch Glut und Rauch.
>
> [I: 67]

To describe these lines as a mixture of Christian and Dionysian elements would be inadequate, inasmuch as such a description is too rational. One is almost left with the impression that the insanity ("Wahnsinn") of the pale priests could apply to the poet as well. In insanity there is also an alteration of the usual perceptive powers. It is symptomatic of schizophrenia that the contours of perceived objects become blurred and distended. Trakl frequently suffered from hallucinations and from childhood on imagined a man standing behind his back with a knife (see II: 730). Although no definite diagnosis of Trakl's mental condition was made during his lifetime, Theodor Spoerri concludes from his investigations that Trakl was probably suffering from "schizophrenia simplex," indicated by certain basic symptoms and a slow "Senkung der Lebenslinie."[26] However, Spoerri is careful to avoid giving the impression that Trakl's poetry stems solely from his probable insanity. Good poetry, he maintains, cannot root entirely in the personality of the poet; it always transcends the poet himself. Moreover, as Spoerri points out, hallucinations can come from other sources and are not automatically a symptom of insanity. Nor do they necessarily indicate a state resulting from the consumption of drugs, which the poet was known to have used. Other modern poets who have been neither mentally ill nor given to the use of narcotics have written poems similar, in their arbitrary, disconnected imagery, to Trakl's.

But even if we concede a hallucinatory condition, produced either through drugs, insanity, or both, as the origin of Trakl's creative impulse, the question remains whether this condition is to be looked upon purely negatively as a mental aberration or positively as a sign of a reality which transcends the poet. Mystics throughout history have been the recipients, sometimes involuntary, of visions the meaning of which both they and others were incapable of grasping. In Christian mysticism, at least, these visions are generally supposed to be the revelations of an infinitely good God, the God of love. But even here there are exceptions. Jakob Böhme, for example, posited a negative principle ("Grimmigkeit") as part of God's essence. From it arose not only the internal activity of the Godhead and all corporeal life, but also the existence of evil and hell. Moreover, the mystics themselves have traditionally stressed that it is not possible to characterize their God by means of any particular attribute; their God could represent just as well the abyss of nothingness as the fullness of essence. (Böhme often used the terms "Nichts" and "Ungrund" to refer to God.)[27] The same basic ambiguity that obtains for mysticism obtains also for Trakl. The interpreter does not really know whether his attempts to understand will lead to an abyss of nothingness or transcendent reality. In Trakl's poetry, at least, one can find abundant evidence for the simultaneous validity of *both* goals.

Another example of what might be considered a hallucinatory flow of images is the poem "Trübsinn":

Weltunglück geistert durch den Nachmittag.
Baraken fliehn durch Gärtchen braun und wüst.
Lichtschnuppen gaukeln um verbrannten Mist,
Zwei Schläfer schwanken heimwärts, grau und vag.

Auf der verdorrten Wiese läuft ein Kind
Und spielt mit seinen Augen schwarz und glatt.
Das Gold tropft von den Büschen trüb und matt.
Ein alter Mann dreht traurig sich im Wind.

Am Abend wieder über meinem Haupt
Saturn lenkt stumm ein elendes Geschick.
Ein Baum, ein Hund tritt hinter sich zurück
Und schwarz schwankt Gottes Himmel und entlaubt.

Ein Fischlein gleitet schnell hinab den Bach;
Und leise rührt des toten Freundes Hand
Und glättet liebend Stirne und Gewand.
Ein Licht ruft Schatten in den Zimmern wach.

[I: 53]

In this poem there seems at first glance to be, rather than a blurring of contours, a careful delineation of the various images. With few ex-

ceptions, each image occupies the space of one single verse, and
little attempt is made to establish a transition from one to another.
The impression left by the entire poem, however, is one of an indis-
tinguishable flurry of activity, of which the individual images are
only the metaphorical approximations. The verbs of this poem serve
to strengthen this impression. Many of them indicate an imprecise
activity, especially in the first stanza: "geistern," "fliehn,"
"gaukeln," "schwanken," and in the last stanza "gleiten." To this list
we can add the verbs "laufen," "drehen," and "treten" if the context
of their appearance is considered. Only the last three lines seem to
offer a relief from this hectic, depressing activity—a relief indicated
by the verbs "rühren" and "glätten."

A more easily demonstrable method by which Trakl maintains a
feeling of uncertainty and ambiguity in his poems is the use of the
words "vielleicht," "oder," and "aber."[28] The word "vielleicht" oc-
curs twice in the poem "Am Rand eines alten Brunnens," which
could also serve as an example of Trakl's random juxtaposition of
images. The poem is one continuous succession of images, ten in all,
appearing in the form of substantives with participial phrase and
relative clause modifiers but no predicates. The whole poem seems
to explicate or illustrate the first four words, "Dunkle Deutung des
Wassers," which are followed by a colon. Here are some lines from
the poem:

> Kammerkonzerte, die auf einer Wendeltreppe verklingen,
> Vielleicht ein Mond, der leise die Stufen hinaufsteigt.
> ....
> Sterne, die auf deine knöchernen Hände fallen,
> Vielleicht ein Gang durch verlassene Zimmer,
>
> [I: 308]

One immediately responds to the inconceivability in the individual
images of a moon climbing the stairs and stars falling upon hands;
still the word "vielleicht" heightens in a pointed way the ambiguity
of this flow of images. Moreover, as these lines show, the individual
images have little to do with one another and certainly do not seem
to be in any way related to the "dark significance of water." The
word "vielleicht" again serves to underline this fact.

The use of the word "oder" is confined largely to the later poetry,
from "Helian" on. It sometimes signals a change of mood as in
"Abendland" where it precedes the appearance of Elis, thus con-
trasting the more optimistic mood of these lines with that of the lines

immediately before. An example of a change of mood in the opposite direction—from the optimistic to the pessimistic—occurs in the first stanza of the fourth section of "Helian":

> Ein erhabenes Schicksal sinnt den Kidron hinab,
> Wo die Zeder, ein weiches Geschöpf,
> Sich unter den blauen Brauen des Vaters entfaltet,
> Über die Weide nachts ein Schäfer seine Herde führt.
> Oder es sind Schreie im Schlaf,
> Wenn ein eherner Engel im Hain den Menschen antritt,
> Das Fleisch des Heiligen auf glühendem Rost hinschmilzt.
>
> [I: 72]

Whatever the context, the word "oder" has the effect of rendering more uncertain both the preceding image or series of images and the new ones suggested in their place.

The use of the word "aber" is especially frequent in the last two prose poems, where a contrast in moods results in uncertainty. In the last section of "Traum und Umnachtung," the changing moods have a tendency to follow upon one another so hastily that the reader is at a loss to distinguish between them. The ending of this section especially, "die Nacht das verfluchte Geschlecht verschlang," casts a pale of gloom over the entire poem. The reader can therefore easily overlook the alternating moods within this section and see only a uniform kind of pessimism. But optimistic interludes are also present, as in the following example signaled by "aber":

> Aber leise sang jener im grünen Schatten des Hollunders, da er aus bösen Träumen erwachte; süsser Gespiele nahte ihm ein rosiger Engel, dass er, ein sanftes Wild, zur Nacht hinschlummerte; und er sah das Sternenantlitz der Reinheit.
>
> [I: 150]

Thus far we have observed methods by which the poet has achieved an absence of concreteness in his poems: the use of verbs and adjectives indicating the blurring of contours; the use of indefinite neuter substantives for human figures; a disconnected, irrational flow of images; and certain words which are more directly indicative of ambiguity (i.e., "vielleicht," "oder," and "aber"). All of these means have to do with the breakdown of reality as we are accustomed to perceive it. In the remainder of this chapter our attention will focus more specifically on how the poet draws together elements which rationally do not belong together: i.e., the use of metaphors in such a way that a basis for comparison is lacking, the transitive use of intransitive verbs, and the use of synesthetic imagery.

A metaphor is usually understood as a comparison, without explicit connecting words such as "like" or "as," between two things which are essentially unalike. There is normally some basis for comparison between the two things, although this basis need not be immediately obvious. In Trakl's poetry metaphors are often used in what might be called an absolute sense, affording no basis at all for the comparison. When Trakl writes of the boy Elis: "Dein Leib ist eine Hyazinthe,/In die ein Mönch die wächsernen Finger taucht" (I: 84), it is difficult to see how one could associate the hyacinth, a flower into which a monk puts his fingers, with the body of Elis. Such a comparison defies logical analysis. The sameness of Trakl's human figures also illustrates his absolute use of metaphors. For example, there is no basis in reality for equating the brother with the sister or the unborn with the deceased.

A particularly striking way in which Trakl frequently uses metaphors involves placing one substantive in apposition to another in such a way that the two substantives appear to be synonymous with each other rather than in a relationship of comparison. In the lines "Einen Zug von wilden Rossen/Blitze grelle Wolken treiben" (I: 27), the reader would expect to see a "wie" in front of "Einen Zug," thus making it a simile for "grelle Wolken" (the bolts of lightning drive the clouds "like" a herd of wild horses). But Trakl omits the "wie" and in so doing allows "Einen Zug von wilden Rossen" to be in apposition to "grelle Wolken." Strictly speaking, "Einen Zug . . ." is neither a simile nor a metaphor in the usual sense. A sentence reading "Blitze treiben einen Zug von wilden Rossen" would provide the usual kind of metaphor. From the incongruity of the situation within the poem the reader would have assumed that the herd of wild horses is representative of something other than itself— something related to the bolts of lightning—namely, the clouds. The metaphorical, i.e., the comparative nature of the image, would have been maintained. Trakl's metaphor, however, suppresses the comparison and makes the herd of wild horses and the clouds appear synonymous.

This type of metaphor is even more striking if there is no basis at all for comparison. In the preceding example the comparison between the clouds and the horses might seem somewhat strained but not at all inconceivable. The imagination of the reader is definitely overtaxed, however, by a sentence like the following: "Eine blaue

Wolke/ist dein Antlitz auf mich gesunken in der Dämmerung" (I: 81). Without the words "dein Antlitz" there would be no problem in understanding the sentence: A blue cloud has descended upon me in the twilight. In Trakl's sentence, however, the blue cloud is in apposition to the countenance, thus complicating the train of thought. In order to see a connection between the cloud and the countenance in this context, one must defy logic by imagining a countenance which descends upon the poet. Through the metaphorical juxtaposition of the two images, Trakl succeeds in rendering the entire sentence ambiguous. But what occurs here is not merely a metaphorical juxtaposition; there is rather a unification of the two images.[29] The blue cloud *is* the countenance and not just "like" the countenance. A mere comparison between the two would have to be called unreal; but their unification surpasses the categories of "real" and "unreal," which are predicated upon a condition of concreteness and individuation, and indicates a condition in which all things are one.

The two images which enter into unification are sometimes not only totally unrelated but even contradictory, as in the following clause from "Jahr": ". . . goldene Wolke/Folgt dem Einsamen, der schwarze Schatten des Enkels" (I: 138). The dead child following the poet (here: "dem Einsamen") is such a familiar motif that the reading of "der schwarze Schatten des Enkels" as the subject of "folgt" comes naturally in spite of the syntax. And since "goldene Wolke" is by syntax also the subject of "folgt," the two images must therefore be synonymous. But now there is the problem of the apparent contradiction involved in equating a black shadow with a golden cloud. This example underlines the injunction against ascribing any absolute values to Trakl's colors. Even golden and black, which have fairly consistent, contrasting values in his poetry—the former positive and the latter negative[30]—can lose their distinctions and become synonymous. The golden cloud *is* the black shadow in spite of the apparent opposition in colors.

In using intransitive verbs such as "schweigen," "rauschen," and "denken" transitively, Trakl also brings together elements which normally do not belong together. For example, the first line of "Im Dunkel" reads: "Es schweigt die Seele den blauen Frühling" (I: 143). Gramatically correct usage would demand either a transitive verb in the place of "schweigt" or the omission of the direct object. Likewise when Trakl writes "Näher rauscht der blaue Quell die Klage der Frauen" (I: 94), the reader would expect to find "singt" or some other transitive verb in place of "rauscht." The same holds true for the following example from "Hohenburg": "Immer denkst du das weisse

Antlitz des Menschen" (I: 87). Either the transitive verb "bedenken" should replace "denken" or "an" should be used before "das weisse Antlitz." In these examples Trakl deliberately disregards correct grammatical usage in order to achieve a particular effect. By altering the intransitive nature of these verbs, the poet has again brought about unity through ambiguity. The reader is unsure of what effects the subjects are supposed to have on their direct objects. The former seem to blend with the latter rather than to act, one upon the other, as separate and distinct grammatical entities. Not only is the soul silent but also the blue springtime. Not only does the blue water murmur but also the lament of the women. Not only does the "du" think but also the white countenance of man. Each image appears to be in apposition to the other rather than in a subject-object relationship.

The frequent use of synesthetic metaphors is a more obvious way in which Trakl causes things to blend together in his poetry.[31] Trakl is by no means the only poet to have made frequent use of such metaphors. Their use was especially common among the German Romantic writers. Synesthesia was extremely compatible with Romantic literary theory which extolled not only the unification of the "genres" but also the mixing of a variety of human expressions in an all-embracing whole, as Friedrich Schlegel calls for in his 116th *Athenäum* Fragment. The poet Novalis writes of such a "mixture" in his *Die Lehrlinge zu Saïs:*

> Es mag lange gedauert haben, ehe die Menschen darauf dachten, die mannichfachen Gegenstände ihrer Sinne mit einem gemeinschaftlichen Namen zu bezeichnen und sich entgegen zu setzen. Durch Uebung werden Entwickelungen befördert, und in allen Entwikkelungen gehen Theilungen, Zergliederungen vor, die man bequem mit den Brechungen des Lichtstrahls vergleichen kann. So hat sich auch nur allmählich unser Innres in so mannichfaltige Kräfte zerspaltet, und mit fortdauernder Uebung wird auch diese Zerspaltung zunehmen. Vielleicht ist es nur krankhafte Anlage der späteren Menschen, wenn sie das Vermögen verlieren, diese zerstreuten Farben ihres Geistes wieder zu mischen und nach Belieben den alten einfachen Naturstand herzustellen, oder neue, mannichfaltige Verbindungen unter ihnen zu bewirken.[32]

The following synesthetic metaphor coming at the end of Trakl's poem "Verklärung" and mixing visual and acoustic impressions is highly reminiscent of Novalis: "Blaue Blume,/Die leise tönt in vergilbtem Gestein" (I: 120). The beginning of the "Prolog" to Goethe's

Faust comes to mind with the following line from Trakl's "Frühling der Seele": "Leise tönt die Sonne im Rosengewölk am Hügel" (I: 141). To these two examples involving the use of the word "tönen" others can be added which bear Trakl's own particular stamp: "Tönendes Grün und Rot" (I: 33); "der Flug der Vögel tönt" (I: 57, 109); "Der Abend tönt in feuchter Bläue fort" (I: 64); "Ein Dornenbusch tönt" (I: 84); "Ach noch tönen von wilden Gewittern die silbernen Arme mir" (I: 168).

A particularly striking example of synesthesia, in which alliteration and assonance also help to create the impression of a perfect blend, is the following line from the poem "Kindheit": "Und in heiliger Bläue läuten leuchtende Schritte fort" (I: 79). The sequence "läuten leuchtende" suggests that the same word is being repeated—almost an internal *rime riche*. Moreover, since these two words indicate acoustic and visual impressions respectively, the near-rhyme tends to stress the synesthetic relationship of the words. Trakl seems to have consciously striven for a blend of elements in his poetry. He even goes as far as to use the rather direct word "mischen" in one synesthetic metaphor: "Leise eine Orgel geht,/Mischet Klang und goldenen Schein," (I: 30).

This chapter has attempted to show that Trakl's poetry does not merely present a succession of independent elements ("Wie schön sich Bild an Bildchen reiht—" [I: 37]), but, through the intimate mingling of these elements, gives an indication of an ultimate reality of unity underlying all things. It is a "mixture" similar to that noted with regard to the incest act in "Passion": "Zwei Wölfe im finsteren Wald / Mischten wir unser Blut in steinerner Umarmung" (I: 393). One must not assume, therefore, that the attainment of unity would automatically entail happiness. Instead it is accompanied by the most negative of circumstances: namely, violence and death. It is the cause for lamenting rather than rejoicing, as Trakl writes at the end of "Nächtliche Klage": "Weh in unendlicher Klage / Mischt sich Feuer, Erde und blauer Quell" (I: 329).

8

The Meaning of Unity

An awareness of the concept of unity is not at all confined to modern times. One can find it in the ancient religions of the East: for example, in the Hindu belief that Atman, the individual soul, and Brahman, the world soul, are identical. In the Western world it formed the central thesis of a philosophical work from the third century A.D., the *Enneads*, in which Plotinus postulated that all visible, material beings arose through emanation from the one ("τὸ ἐν") and that in man's soul a counterthrust toward reunion with the one becomes effective. The important tenets of Plotinus were carried over into the mysticism of the Middle Ages and are especially apparent in Meister Eckhart's formulation of the *unio mystica* experience. In the seventeenth century Benedict Spinoza, influenced by Jewish mysticism and Neoplatonic thought, again proclaimed the union of the natural and the supernatural ("Deus sive natura"). His work, in turn, had a profound influence on Lessing, Goethe, and the German Romanticists. Goethe, who acknowledged his own belief in a kind of "pantheism," bore witness to Spinoza's influence in the statement that Spinoza, together with Shakespeare and Linné, had had the greatest effect on his development (H.A., XIII: 562).

Nor can the concept of unity be restricted to modern poetry as opposed to older poetry. In the chapter entitled "Die Erfahrung der Einheitswirklichkeit" of his book *Der schöpferische Mensch*, Erich Neumann points out that all true works of art give evidence of a region that is neither internal to man nor external, but one that

transcends and unifies both man and the world.[33] However, the
same author also indicates that the idea of unity might be mani-
festing itself with more insistence and urgency in our own time than
in the past.

> Das Dilemma, in dem wir als moderne Menschen leben, besteht darin,
> dass wir als westliche Menschen den anthropozentrischen Akzent
> nicht verlieren können und nicht verlieren dürfen. Aber wir sind in
> unserer Entwicklung zu einer so übermässigen Zentrierung im Ich
> gekommen, dass wir durch diese Überbetonung des Ich in die Gefahr
> des Zerfalls unserer polarisierten Welt geraten sind. Weil wir in einen
> fast unversöhnlichen Gegensatz von Mensch und Natur, Ich und
> Selbst, Bewusstsein und Unbewusstem hineingeraten sind, taucht
> heute die Gegenkonstellation der Einheitswirklichkeit mit um so stär-
> kerer und Erlösung bringender Kraft auf. Deswegen bewegt sich etwas
> in uns vom im Ich zentrierten Nur-Menschlichen fort und zum gros-
> sen Anthropos, dem Adam Kadmon, hin, in dem Menschliches und
> Welthaftes noch nicht auseinandergetreten sind, und aus diesem
> Grunde drängt in uns etwas zur Erfahrung der Ganzheit und Einheit-
> lichkeit, mehr vielleicht als in anderen Zeiten. Deswegen spielt für
> die Moderne nicht nur der schöpferische Mensch eine Rolle, die er
> sonst im Bewusstsein einer Zeit nie besessen hat, sondern ebenso
> auch das Kind und der "einfache" Mensch. In ihrer durch kein Be-
> wusstsein gestörten Ganzheit ist die Erfahrung der Einheitswirklich-
> keit stumm, aber lebendig, und die Sympathie aller belebten und
> unbelebten Dinge hat sich in ihnen noch wach und strahlend erhal-
> ten.[34]

In modern times man has begun to realize that a great split has
developed in the world. Through his expanding consciousness, man
has become more and more separated from the world which sur-
rounds him. Although enhancing man's capabilities beyond the
imagination of previous centuries, this expanding consciousness has
at the same time put man in the terrifying position of standing alone
in a world of his own making for which he bears total responsibility.
Psychology, especially the depth psychology of C. G. Jung, has made
man increasingly aware of the intolerable situation in which he
stands. The pendulum which, since the Middle Ages, has swung in
the direction of the glorification of the individual man and the insist-
ence upon his absolute freedom with respect to his surroundings—to
mold them or destroy them as he sees fit—is now beginning to swing
back in the opposite direction. Man is troubled more and more by a
sense of loss: the loss of the totality of which he was once a part.

Gottfried Benn, a contemporary of Trakl's who outlived him by four decades, sees the development of man in a similar light. In his lecture "Das moderne Ich," Benn depicts the over-individuated man, the absolute subject, as ripe for transition to a new form of existence, in a world without concreteness, without the separation of subject from object. It is the hour, Benn declares: "—nun ist die Stunde der grossen Nacht, des Rausches und der entwichenen Formen."[35] And then, in an interesting parallel to Trakl, Benn goes on to tell his listeners who the new man is. He is Narcissus, the self-centered individual who has succeeded in breaking through the prison of his individuality to experience himself in the totality of nature.

> Aber es sind Felder über der Erde, die tragen nichts als Blumen des Rausches—halt an, Narziss, es starben die Moiren, mit den Menschen sprichst du wie mit Wind—, wie weit du fühltest, wie weit du spültest, dir ward dein eignes lyäisches Bild.[36]

Trakl's frequent use of the Narcissus motif indicates this same desire for wholeness. It is a wholeness to be achieved by pushing the irreversible process of individuation to the farthest extent possible— to a point at which the individual will cease to be an individual and will manifest himself as the world. For Benn as for Trakl, this process involves death: not a death which lies ominously in wait for man at the end of life, but rather one which informs life throughout:

> Wenn wir aber lehrten den Reigen sehen und das Leben formend überwinden, würde da der Tod nicht sein der Schatten, blau, in dem die Glücke stehen?
>   Des Endens Süsse, des Vergängnisses Rausch; um jeden Abend der Schimmer des letzten, durch jede Stunde das orphische Ermatten, des Sinkens Schauer, der Sichheit grauenvolles Glück?[37]

The concept of Regression in Benn's writings must be understood in a twofold way. It is a step backward into the primitive; but it is, at the same time, a step forward into the desired state of totality, the future of man. Benn distinguishes between two classes of men: those who adhere to totality and those who adhere to the preeminence of the individual. He places himself among the former, along with the other "Expressionisten,"[38] including Trakl.[39] The style of Expressionism derives, in Benn's words, from a basic inclination toward "Wirklichkeitszertrümmerung," an attempt to experience a reality "nicht mehr individuell und sensualistisch gefärbt."[40]

Jung refers to the reality beyond individuation as "unus mundus," a term he borrows from an alchemic work, the "Physica Trismegisti" of Gerard Dorn.[41] The "unus mundus" was the world immediately after its creation by God and before its division into two regions, heaven and earth, and the ensuing multiplicity of things. The final step of the alchemic process was to be a reunion of the adept with the "unus mundus," the world of nondifferentiated unity. If this notion appears "mystic," it is, as Jung claims, due to an ignorance of the nature of the psyche.[42] The psychic is not something completely independent of the physical; rather the two interpenetrate each other. In the area of interpenetration the psychic can no longer be considered purely psychic nor the physical purely physical. Jung postulates the existence of a third state encompassing the other two, to which he applies the designation "unus mundus." He is careful to emphasize that the precise nature of the "one world" will always escape the grasp of human reason, but he insists on maintaining it as a "probable hypothesis" to explain some of the findings not only of depth psychology but of microphysics as well.[43] In both science and psychology there is an increasing abundance of evidence indicating the identity of the psychic and the physical and in a more general sense, therefore, of man and the outside world.

The French literary scholar Albert Béguin considers the union of subject and object to be an essential characteristic of modern poetry in particular. In his essay entitled "Poésie et mystique," he points out that French poetry since Romanticism, and especially since Rimbaud, has tended to become more and more irrational while at the same time being highly cognizant of its irrationality.[44] French poetry has consciously moved in a direction resembling the magical activities of primitive peoples and the efforts of the mystics—in short, in the direction of the occultist tradition:

> Mots en liberté, écriture automatique, tant de tentatives récentes reposent sur une croyance qui appartient à la tradition occultiste: croyance en une analogie profonde entre la nature extérieure et la structure du monde intérieur.[45]

Just as the mystic, in descending to the uttermost depths of his soul, hopes to be united with the divine spirit, so the modern poet, in allowing a completely free rein to an exaggerated subjectivity, in fostering an arbitrary experimentation with language and images, hopes to achieve admission to a region which surpasses the subject:

> Ainsi se forme l'étrange espoir d'atteindre, précisément par le subjectivisme absolu, à la seule objectivité valable: c'est au terme de la descente en soi, alors qu'il n'accepte plus que ce qui est unique et

personnel, que l'homme prétend saisir enfin quelque chose qui le dépasse.[46]

The arbitrary flow of diverse images in modern poetry lets one sense a unity beyond the apparent multiplicity of things.[47] In this union with that which surpasses the individual, modern poetry and mysticism are on common ground.[48]

Walther Killy, too, seems to recognize that Trakl's poetry points to a reality beyond the grasp of the intellect and cannot, therefore, be considered a mere aesthetic game with disconnected images. Just before a quotation from Albert Béguin's essay, Killy writes of Trakl's style:

> Es handelt sich nicht um ein bloss ästhetisches Spiel voller Unverbindlichkeit, mag sein Reiz noch so gross sein. Es geht um die Herstellung des Raums für jenes letzte Unbegreifliche. Das ist der Grund für die "Armut" an Ausdrücken und Wendungen, die . . . immer neu variiert werden. Bei allem geht es um *eine* verborgene Wahrheit.[49]

Killy's statement, however, runs contrary to his other conclusions, both in *Wandlungen des lyrischen Bildes* and elsewhere in *Über Georg Trakl*, where he stresses the hopelessness of Trakl's disintegrating world and his purely aesthetic mastery of the situation, his "Spiel" with images. For example, in the former Killy writes:

> [Trakl] hatte in sich ein "infernalisches Chaos von Rhythmen und Bildern," die er verabsolutierte. Die Bilder bleiben bestehen, aber das Spiel mit ihnen geschieht nicht mehr im Hinblick auf die Wirklichkeit.[50]

In *Über Georg Trakl* Killy quotes from Trakl's letter to Ludwig von Ficker in which the poet expresses his despair over his disintegrating world (I: 530).[51] Applying this quotation to Trakl's poetry, Killy concludes that there is no connection between the various images, that the poems are testimony to a lack of communication and general hopelessness. "Es gehört nicht mehr zusammen, sondern es steht alles einzeln für sich da, in grausamem Auseinanderfall."[52] The poet takes the elements of a chaotic world and strives to achieve with them an aesthetic order which is effective only within the confines of the poem itself.

> Dagegen wird nun das Gedicht gestellt, und zwar so, dass es das Chaos nicht aufhebt—das kann es nicht—, aber zu bändigen sucht. Es

greift dazu auf ursprüngliche Mittel zurück. Der Kunstverstand sucht sich zu erobern, was das Schicksal entzieht. Hat die Welt keine einsehbare Ordnung oder ist diese, obwohl sehnsüchtig erinnert, dem geschichtlichen Augenblick vorenthalten, so sucht das Gedicht sie herzustellen, und zwar auf die bescheidenste und älteste Weise: scheinbar spielend—nicht aber Sinn setzend. Dies "Spiel" mit den Elementen der Welt ist eine überaus ernste Sache, tröstlich schon, wenn sich die Widersprüche für die Dauer der Verse ins Verhältnis bringen lassen.[53]

This remains the major theme of Killy's 1960s' Trakl research. In his article for the *Festschrift für Bernhard Blume* entitled "Bestand und Bewegung in Gedichten Georg Trakls," Killy maintains that while a yearning for the truth concerns and motivates Trakl, in the chaotic world of the present this "truth" is to be found only in the certitude of never knowing it. The resulting frustration explains the vague, often contradictory elements of his poetry. Trakl, according to Killy, strives in desperation to overcome the "Chaos" of the real world in the "Kosmos" of *aesthetic* production.[54]

The inadequacy of Killy's approach lies in the fact that although he gives occasional hints of a base underlying the disconnected and distorted imagery of Trakl's poetry (e.g., "jenes letzte Unbegreifliche"), he fails to give due emphasis to this base. For Killy, the disintegration of the traditionally conceived reality is of prime importance, not the signs of a new world emerging through the broken pieces of the old. This new world, however, cannot be the merely aesthetic production of the poet, valid only for his poetry. On the contrary, the poetry itself reflects the increasingly evident existence of the new world, the world of unity.

The unity which has been the focal point of this study manifests itself in the final analysis as the union of subject and object. In this union Trakl's poetry is not at all unique as far as modern poetry is concerned. Rimbaud wrote "*Je* est un autre"; and in his poetry, too, the poetic subject is dissolved in the flow of images.[55] The critical attempts to prove Trakl's indebtedness to Rimbaud, including Herbert Lindenberger's *Georg Trakl*, have, until now, failed to appreciate the aspect of Rimbaud's art related to mysticism. For them, Trakl continues in the purely "l'art pour l'art" tradition established by Rimbaud and the French Symbolists. In this sense, such critical evaluations fall into the same category as Killy's interpretation of Trakl's poetry. Moreover, none of them takes into account the major thematic patterns of incest and death which bear Trakl's own particular stamp and are not to be found as such in Rimbaud's work.

There is, however, another parallel to the concept of unity as illustrated in Trakl's poetry. Perhaps one of the most profound and striking experiences of twentieth-century man is the way the world surrounding him is rapidly coming together to form a cohesive unit. This cohesion is the result of unprecedented advances in the fields of transportation and communications. To the rapidly converging world of present civilization, Erich Fromm applies the designation "One World," which must be distinguished from Jung's "unus mundus," the nondifferentiated world of pure potency as it was supposed to have existed immediately after creation. Fromm points out that long before humanity began to experience "One World," advanced thinkers had formulated the concept of "One Man" (i.e., the basic equality of all men). This concept remained the luxury of speculative thought until the present, but now it must be put into practice if the "One World" is to survive. Fromm, therefore, conceives the "One World" and "One Man" not as hypothetical postulates of psychology but as present reality and the demand of present reality respectively.[56] Going a step farther, Pierre Teilhard de Chardin, the Jesuit scientist-philosopher, sees all of evolution as a process in which the force of convergence plays a dominant role. After the beginnings of consciousness in man, this force accelerated and will lead eventually to the union of all men and with them the rest of creation in the person of Christ, the "Omega point," the goal of evolution.[57] In this connection, Trakl's resurrected "*Ein Geschlecht*" comes to mind as an allusion not only to a union of the sexes but also to the union of all men in one race.

For Romano Guardini, "One Man" is already here in the form of "Mass Man."[58] The "modern" world, which lasted roughly from the time of the Renaissance to just after the turn of the present century, was characterized by a cult of the personality and a veneration of nature as a benevolent force. Both man and nature were considered as absolutes, in contrast to the older belief in an absolute divinity which directed both man and nature to their respective ends. Goethe, in his life and work, gave the most complete expression to the "modern" concept of man and nature. The "post-modern man," however, the man of this century, no longer experiences himself as an independent personality, but rather as part of an anonymous mass servicing an all-encompassing technology which has proven to be the instrument not only of tremendous advancement but also of unbelievable destruction. No longer considered an independent entity worthy of veneration and affording in its permanence security to man, nature, too, has come completely under the sway of a morally ambivalent technology. Present-day man, without a secure place in a world of his own making, is plagued by a dreadful anxiety in the face of an ever-growing danger.

> Science and technology have so mastered the forces of nature that destruction, either chronic or acute and incalculable in extent, is now a possibility. Without exaggeration one can say that a new era of history has been born. Now and forever man will live at the brink of an ever-growing danger which shall leave its mark upon his entire existence.[59]

The act of subduing nature was itself a manifestation of nature, namely in the form of man's power. In this form nature again rises to threaten man in ways more terrifying than in primitive times.

> The wildernesses of nature have long been under the control of man; nature as it exists round and about us obeys its master. Nature now, however, has emerged once again into history from within the very depths of culture itself. Nature is rising up in that very form which subdued the wilderness—in the form of power itself. All the abysses of primeval ages yawn before man, all the wild, choking growth of the long-dead forests presses forward from this second wilderness, all the monsters of the desert wastes, all the horrors of darkness are once more upon man. He stands again before chaos, a chaos more dreadful than the first because most men go their own complacent ways without seeing, because scientifically-educated gentlemen everywhere deliver their speeches as always, because the authorities function as usual.[60]

And yet in spite of all this Guardini can see in the new age signs of hope springing from a realistic acceptance of conditions as they are without deceptive embellishment, conditions which include the unity of "Mass Man."[61]

Trakl's poetry shows that he was very aware of the realities of what Guardini was later to call the "post-modern" world. Nature in Trakl's poetry, far from being a secure refuge for man, is itself involved in the universal process of decay and destruction. Many of the images of Trakl's later poetry are prophecies of the actual desolation which was soon to be visited upon civilization—prophecies spoken in an atmosphere of complacency comparable to that which, in Guardini's analysis, blinds present-day man to the dangers surrounding him. The following examples are all from poems written before the outbreak of World War I.

Dunklere Tränen odmet diese Zeit,
Verdammnis, da des Träumers Herz
Überfliesst von purpurner Abendröte,
Der Schwermut der rauchenden Stadt;

[I: 132]

Ihr sterbenden Völker!
Bleiche Woge
Zerschellend am Strande der Nacht,
Fallende Sterne.

[I: 140]

Aufflattern weisse Vögel am Nachtsaum
Über stürzenden Städten
Von Stahl.

[I: 156]

Ihr Soldaten!
Vom Hügel, wo sterbend die Sonne rollt
Stürzt das lachende Blut—
Unter Eichen
Sprachlos! O grollende Schwermut
Des Heers; ein strahlender Helm
Sank klirrend von purpurner Stirne.

[I:161]

The last stanza of the poem "Im Osten," written shortly before Trakl was to leave for the Russian front in August 1914 (see II: 310), speaks metaphorically of a wilderness surrounding civilization, bringing to mind Guardini's "second wilderness," a wilderness about to break into man's secure domain.

Dornige Wildnis umgürtet die Stadt.
Von blutenden Stufen jagt der Mond
Die erschrockenen Frauen.
Wilde Wölfe brachen durchs Tor.

[I: 165]

The poet's search for unity shows signs of ending in total annihilation. His is an anxiety which reflects the threatened existence of all mankind, as expressed in his next-to-last poem, "Klage": "Des Menschen goldnes Bildnis/ Verschlänge die eisige Woge/Der Ewigkeit" (I: 166). And yet even among these last poems there is one whose key word is hope. Entitled "Die Heimkehr," it was written in June 1914 and published posthumously in the Brenner Jahrbuch of

1915 (see II: 302). It tells of a hope to return home: first of all, back in
time to the innocence of "crystal childhood" and the love that awaits
the poet there (the sister?),[62] but also forward to the final abode of
death. Here again is an illustration of the circular nature of Trakl's
poetry, the circle of death. It is not, however, the frightening death of
annihilation but a welcome death heralded by the words "Glaube,
Hoffnung!"

> Die Kühle dunkler Jahre,
> Schmerz und Hoffnung
> Bewahrt zyklopisch Gestein,
> Menschenleeres Gebirge,
> Des Herbstes goldner Odem,
> Abendwolke—
> Reinheit!
>
> Anschaut aus blauen Augen
> Kristallne Kindheit;
> Unter dunklen Fichten
> Liebe, Hoffnung,
> Dass von feurigen Lidern
> Tau ins starre Gras tropft—
> Unaufhaltsam!
>
> O! dort der goldene Steg
> Zerbrechend im Schnee
> Des Abgrunds!
> Blaue Kühle
> Odmet das nächtige Tal,
> Glaube, Hoffnung!
> Gegrüsst du einsamer Friedhof!

[I: 162]

Notes

Complete publication data can be found in the Selected
Bibliography.

Introduction

1. Szklenar, *Erinnerung an Georg Trakl*, pp. 8–9.
2. Lachmann's interpretation of "Passion" in his *Kreuz und Abend* was criticized
by Walther Killy in "Das Spiel des Orpheus. Über die erste Fassung von Georg Trakls
'Passion,' " *Euphorion* 51 (1957): 422–37 (later reprinted in *Über Georg Trakl*, pp. 21–
37). Lachmann answered Killy in "Georg Trakls herbstliche 'Passion.' " Killy con-
tinued the argument in "Nochmals über Trakls 'Passion.' "
3. E.g., Dietz, *Die lyrische Form Georg Trakls;* Magnuson, "Consonant Repetition in
the Lyric of Georg Trakl"; Preisendanz, "Auflösung und Verdinglichung in den
Gedichten Georg Trakls"; Wetzel, *Klang und Bild in den Dichtungen Georg Trakls;*
Schier, "Von den Metaphern zur figuralen Sprache, Abgrenzung der Begriffe"; Kem-
per, *Georg Trakls Entwürfe;* Philipp, *Die Funktion des Wortes in den Gedichten Georg
Trakls;* Lindenberger, *Georg Trakl;* Bolli, *Georg Trakls "Dunkler Wohllaut".* Although
Kemper and Bolli claim to move away from Killy's position, they remain essentially
bound to it. Kemper expends much critical effort in arriving at meager conclusions on
the basis of Trakl's earlier drafts. Bolli's adherence to Killy's position is indicated by
the following statement: "Trakls Existenz wäre mit dem Zerbrechen der Welt dem
Untergang ausgeliefert, wenn nicht aus der Tiefe seiner Einbildungskraft eine Har-
monie ertönte, die den Wirklichkeitsfragmenten im Kunstwerk einen Zusammenhang
verliehe" (*Georg Trakls "Dunkler Wohllaut,"* p. 78; see also pp. 76 and 154). An
exception to this trend is Hellmich's *Klang und Erlösung*, reminiscent of Lachmann's
critical approach and equally unconvincing.
4. The relations between Ludwig von Ficker and Trakl will be explored in a book
which I am currently preparing under the title *Georg Trakl and the Brenner Circle*.
5. Killy, *Über Georg Trakl*, pp. 21, 34.
6. Ibid., p. 37.
7. Ibid., p. 35.
8. See Killy, *Wandlungen des lyrischen Bildes*, pp. 119ff.

9. Trakl, *Dichtungen und Briefe*, I: 530. (Hereafter all references to this edition will be indicated in the text by volume and page number.) These words of Trakl's have been cited by Killy and other critics as central to the understanding of his poetry.

10. Gustav Kars calls for, and in specific instances points the way to, the kind of interpretation I have attempted. See his "Georg Trakl in wechselnder Deutung."

11. A recent book by Francis Michael Sharp entitled *The Poet's Madness*, in apparent disregard of Goldmann's previous work on this subject, applies the psychiatric theories of R. D. Laing to Trakl's poetry and finds in it signs of "reintegration as well as disintegration" (p. 193). In spite of the above-mentioned oversight, this book provides a welcome exception in Trakl criticism to the dominant direction of excessive attention to form exclusive of meaning.

12. Heidegger, "Eine Erörterung von Georg Trakls Gedicht" in *Unterwegs zur Sprache*, pp. 37–82.

13. A recent example of the latter is Palmier's ambitious undertaking, *Situation de Georg Trakl*.

Part I

1. Spoerri, *Georg Trakl*, p. 41. Trakl's only biographer of note also leaves little doubt that Trakl's relationship with his sister involved incest; see Basil, "Die Fremdlingin" in *Georg Trakl in Selbstzeugnissen und Bilddokumenten*, pp. 70–84.

2. Hamburger, *Reason and Energy*, p. 242.

3. See Killy's statement in *Über Georg Trakl*: "In der Liebe zur Schwester verwirklicht sich die Erfahrung äusserster Schuld. Nur ein bigotter Moralismus oder psychologisierende Neugier können darin etwas anders als die stellvertretend erlittene Unordnung erblicken, die zur grossen, metaphysisch gerichteten Unruhe wird" (p. 26).

4. Ibid., pp. 21–37.

5. I: 119. This poem was written in December 1913 in Innsbruck (see II: 203). The *Brenner* version of "Passion" was written at the beginning of 1914, also in Innsbruck (see II: 218), thus establishing a close link in terms of time.

6. Killy's injunction against attaching any constant frame of reference to Trakl's often fluctuating images does not obtain in this particular case. In other instances it seems, at first glance, to be valid. The word "Stern" in the poem "Passion," for instance, is associated with Christ's birth in line 20 ("Sternenfrost des Winters"), with incest in line 37 ("die Sterne unseres Geschlechts"), and with the redemption and regeneration of the lovers in line 53 ("die sanfte Sternenstunde"). But even here, the series of events in its entirety must take precedence over each single event to which the image "Stern" attaches. If the outcome of the series is positive, even the individual negative events of the series take on, with their accompanying images, something of this positive value.

7. Killy, *Über Georg Trakl*, p. 34.

8. I cannot agree with Walter Falk's interpretation of these lines in *Leid und Verwandlung*. He speaks of the boy being incestuously drawn to his mother: "Aber genauer besehen, sagt das Gedicht, der Knabe 'erglühe' der Mutter und zwar 'purpurn'. . . . Und der 'Knabe' ist zwar das Kind der Mutter, aber in eins damit auch ein Mensch, über den 'Weh' gerufen wird, weil er seine Mutter zum Weibe begehrt" (p. 336). In order to achieve his reading of "schmerzlicher Mutter" as a dative depending on "erglüht," Falk overlooks the fact that there is a comma between the two in Trakl's text. I consider "schmerzlicher Mutter" as a genitive parallel to "der schmalen

Gestalt des Knaben," a genitive depending on the exclamation "Weh." In other words, "Weh" is also to be read before "schmerzlicher Mutter," thus separating it from the preceding relative clause "die purpurn erglüht." Moreover, if one were to follow Falk's interpretation, this would be the only time in his works that Trakl makes reference to a mother-son incest, all other references being to the brother-sister type.

9. Walther Killy does not recognize the possibility of identifying the "du" and does not acknowledge its death until line 25 ("Ein Leichnam suchest du unter grünenden Bäumen"). In Über Georg Trakl he writes: "War zunächst eine an ein unbestimmtes Du gerichtete Frage gestellt worden, so ist nun das Du tot . . . während die Bäume grünen" (p. 24). The "du" does not appear dead first in line 25 but already in line 3 ("Wer bist du Ruhendes unter hohen Bäumen?"), which echoes "ein Totes" of line 2: Nor does the "du" remain "unbestimmt," as Killy indicates, until line 25; it is already identified as the boy in line 13.

10. This explanation of "härene Höhle" does not preclude the possible validity of Falk's interpretation: "Die 'härene Höhle' wäre so als Raum des Geschlechtlichen zu verstehen" Leid und Verwandlung, p. 340.

11. Goldmann, Katabasis, pp. 142–43, 150. Cf. also the already quoted lines from "Frühling der Seele" (I: 141), pp. 10–11.

12. Basil, Georg Trakl in Selbstzeugnissen, p. 78.

13. Trakl's attitude in this regard is again ambivalent. In a sentence from "Traum und Umnachtung" he seems to adopt a more conciliatory attitude toward his addiction: "Silbern blühte der Mohn auch, trug in grüner Kapsel unsere nächtigen Sternenträume" (I: 150).

14. Novalis, Schriften, I: 368.

15. See, for example, "Helian": "Am Abend begegnen sich Auferstandene auf Felsenpfaden" (I: 72).

16. See Rilke, Briefe aus Muzot: "Der Engel der Elegien ist dasjenige Geschöpf, in dem die Verwandlung des Sichtbaren in Unsichtbares, die wir leisten, schon vollzogen erscheint. . . . Der Engel der Elegien ist dasjenige Wesen, das dafür einsteht, im Unsichtbaren einen höheren Rang der Realität zu erkennen" (p. 337).

17. Another such color is blue, which is most frequently associated with an aura of sublimity and holiness, or at least a kind of mollifying calmness, e.g., "Nachtlied" (I: 68). See also Goldmann's discussion of the significance of blue in Trakl's poetry (Katabasis, pp. 29–33).

18. E.g., the last sentence of "Winternacht" ("Aus dem östlichen Tor trat silbern der rosige Tag" [I: 128]) and line 46 of "Sebastian im Traum" ("Rosige Osterglocke im Grabgewölbe der Nacht" [I: 90]).

19. See also Goldmann, Katabasis, p. 48.

20. Note the frequent use of the word "dunkel" (four times) and "schwarz" (three times) in this poem, also "finster" (once). "Dunkel" is the most frequently used adjective in all of Trakl's poetry. See the "Häufigkeitsliste" in Wetzel, Konkordanz zu den Dichtungen Georg Trakls, p. 813.

21. See Heselhaus, "Die Elis-Gedichte von Georg Trakl," pp. 384–413, esp. 384–86. Heselhaus, however, does not believe that Trakl's "hermetische Dichtung" is completely impenetrable, especially in the case of the Elis poems.

22. The line numbers here and in the following passages refer to the numbering of the critical edition.

23. Lachmann, Kreuz und Abend, pp. 216–32.

24. "Georg Trakl's 'Traum und Umnachtung." Sharp in The Poet's Madness also devotes considerable space to Trakl's last two prose poems (pp. 147–59). Although his

conclusions are in general similar to mine, he does not recognize an intensification of the transformative elements in "Offenbarung und Untergang" as compared to "Traum und Umnachtung."

25. Often when there is clear indication of incest accompanied by a reference to place in Trakl's works, the outdoors is mentioned in some form. It is either the park as in "Traum des Bösen" (I: 29), the forest as in "Passion" and "Frühling der Seele" (I: 141), or the garden as in the above cited instances. It is tempting to speculate that some of the incestuous acts may have occurred or been imagined in the outdoors, perhaps in the garden of the Trakl family in Salzburg, perhaps even in the garden house in which the children played, the picture of which appears in Basil's *Georg Trakl in Selbstzeugnissen*, p. 41. The poet also frequently seems to indicate that the incestuous relationship began fairly early in his life. I have not seen these possibilities discussed in any of the secondary literature of a biographical nature.

26. Lamplight is generally a positive image in Trakl's poetry, even tending to conjure up the sanctuary light of a church: e.g., in the last stanza of "In den Nachmittag geflüstert":

> Dämmerung voll Ruh und Wein;
> Traurige Gitarren rinnen.
> Und zur milden Lampe drinnen
> Kehrst du wie im Traume ein.

                                              [I: 54]

27. Heidegger, *Unterwegs zur Sprache*, pp. 48–49.

28. See I: 425, line 4: "Da aus Sebastians Schatten die verstorbene Schwester trat."

29. See "Abendländisches Lied" (I: 119). The first stanza, with its pastoral existence and its sacrificial rites, contains allusions to an early period of man's history: "Hirten gingen wir einst an dämmernden Wäldern hin" and "Blut blühend am Opferstein." The next two stanzas contain images which refer more specifically to the Christian era: "O, ihr Kreuzzüge und glühenden Martern/Des Fleisches . . ."; "Da wir friedliche Mönche die purpurne Traube gekeltert"; "O, ihr Jagden und Schlösser"; and "Da in seiner Kammer der Mensch Gerechtes sann,/In stummem Gebet um Gottes lebendiges Haupt rang."

30. Tieck reports from Novalis' notes for the continuation of *Heinrich von Ofterdingen*: "Menschen, Thiere, Pflanzen, Steine und Gestirne, Elemente, Töne, Farben, kommen zusammen wie Eine Familie, handeln und sprechen wie Ein Geschlecht" (Novalis, *Schriften*, I: 368). Here, of course, "Geschlecht" is to be considered as race.

"Abendländisches Lied" abounds in possible allusions to Novalis' novel. The beginning of the poem evokes the harmony of man and nature which Novalis also sees as past and future events: "Hirten gingen wir einst an dämmernden Wäldern hin/Und es folgte das rote Wild, die grüne Blume und der lallende Quell/Demutsvoll." "Blut blühend am Opferstein" corresponds to the stone on which the "Blue Flower" sacrifices herself in the transformation of Heinrich. An even more literal correspondence to Novalis' "Blue Flower," also called "Cyane," is in the verse: "O, das sanfte Zyanenbündel der Nacht." "Kreuzzüge," "friedliche Mönche," and "Jagden und Schlösser" correspond to the medieval setting of Novalis' novel. No thorough study of the correspondences between Novalis and Trakl has yet been made. (See Saas, *Georg Trakl*, p. 63.)

31. See Szklenar," *Erinnerung an Georg Trakl*, pp. 117–26. Carl Dallago, a member of the *Brenner* circle from South Tirol and chief contributor to the periodical, was

supposed to have introduced Trakl to the writings of Kierkegaard (Basil, *Georg Trakl in Selbstzeugnissen*, p. 12). Limbach was a Swiss author who had spent some time in Russia.

32. This had not always been Trakl's attitude toward Nietzsche. Earlier in his life he had been an admirer of Nietzsche and is reported to have read from Nietzsche's poetry to the literary circle he frequented. One of his early poems, "Das tiefe Lied" (I: 228), shows a close resemblance to Nietzsche's "Das trunkene Lied" from *Also sprach Zarathustra*.

33. Szklenar, *Erinnerung an Georg Trakl*, p. 124 (italics in Limbach's text).

34. Ibid., p. 118.

35. Heidegger, *Unterwegs zur Sprache*, p. 76.

36. Ibid.

37. See Focke, S. J., *Georg Trakl. Liebe und Tod.*

38. Salomon Reinach, *Cultes, mythes, et religions*, I: 451–58.

39. Weininger, *Geschlecht und Charakter*, pp. 468, 606–7n. See also Doppler, "Georg Trakl und Otto Weininger," in *Peripherie und Zentrum*, pp. 43–52, esp. 51.

40. Reinach, *Cultes, mythes, et religions*, I: 453.

41. Ibid., I: 455–56.

42. Ibid., I: 456–58.

43. Novalis, *Schriften*, I: 318.

44. Schlegel, *Dichtungen*, V: 12–13.

45. Böhme, *Sämtliche Schriften*, II: 258.

46. Reitzenstein and Schraeder, *Studien zum antiken Synkretismus aus Iran und Griechenland*, pp. 9–11.

47. Ibid., pp. 17, 21.

48. Böhme, *Sämtliche Schriften*, II: 250.

49. Szklenar, *Erinnerung an Georg Trakl*, pp. 121–22.

50. Spoerri, *Georg Trakl*, p. 23.

51. Neumann, *Der schöpferische Mensch*, p. 251.

52. Mörike, *Werke*, I: 86–87.

53. Delcourt, *Hermaphrodite*, p. xi.

54. Ibid., pp. 17–32. On the island of Cyprus, for example, a deity called "Aphroditos" was worshiped. It had a woman's body and clothing, but the beard and sexual organs of a man. In the ritual of worship, a kind of fertility rite, transvestism was practiced by both men and women worshipers (p. 27).

55. Ibid., pp. 33–42. Two of these legends involve mortal beings who pass through successive stages of masculinity and femininity and achieve a certain immortality. Kaineus, originally Kainis, the daughter of a king, becomes a man and a tyrant. Kaineus is conquered by the power of Zeus and is buried beneath a mass of tree trunks but nevertheless remains alive and invulnerable in the earth (pp. 35–36). Tiresias, the blind soothsayer who spends part of his life as a woman, lives to an extreme old age (seven or nine generations) and is, even in Hades, the only shade permitted to retain his sense perception and intellectual faculties (pp. 36–39). Delcourt also cites the legend of the Phoenix, the bird which, through its death and rebirth in fire, became a symbol of immortality; it too was endowed with androgynous characteristics (p. 36).

56. Critics have been tempted to see in Trakl a man who would be thoroughly opposed to the war, especially if we assume that it represents an imperialistic instrument of the dying culture he so often decries in his poetry. But the fact is that prior to the war he had personally sought reactivation in the army as a medic. When the war finally broke out Trakl, who came from a typically bourgeois, patriotic Austrian fam-

ily, seems actually to have welcomed it as a solution to his problems (Basil, *Georg Trakl in Selbst*, p. 145).

57. Delcourt, *Hermaphrodite*, pp. 93–99.

58. Reitzenstein and Schraeder, *Studium zum antiken Synkretismus*, p. 229, n. 3. Gayomard is born of a union between Ohrmazd, who corresponds to the Christian God, and Spandarmad, his daughter, the spirit of the earth. Gayomard, in turn, produces the first human pair through a union with his mother, Spandarmad. This pair, who are, of course, brother and sister, then unite to give rise to the human race. Thus here at the beginning of the race all three forms of incest occur.

59. Rank, *Das Inzest-Motiv.*

60. Ibid., pp. 443ff.

61. Ibid., pp. 681–85.

62. Jung, *Mysterium Coniunctionis*, p. 466.

63. Jung, "The Psychology of the Transference," in *The Practice of Psychotherapy*, pp. 229–30.

64. Ibid., pp. 233–34.

65. See the chapter "Die Schwester," pp. 122–55, esp. 150.

66. The words *"Ein Geschlecht,"* as the reader may recall, come at the end of the poem "Abendländisches Lied" with its allusions to the history of Western man. Although there are no further indications of the unity of humanity in Trakl's poetry, Karl Röck, Trakl's friend and co-contributor to the *Brenner*, has recorded in his diary several conversations with Trakl which make the latter's attitude in this regard clear. In one conversation from the summer of 1913 Trakl rebuked Röck for his prejudice against Jews and blacks. According to Röck, Trakl viewed the differences among the races as unimportant (Röck, *Tagebuch 1891–1946*, I: 239–40).

67. Jung, *Psychology and Alchemy*, pp. 327–39, 346–52. See also Jung, *The Practice of Psychotherapy*, pp. 200–330.

68. Jung, *The Practice of Psychotherapy*, p. 275.

69. Wetzel, *Klang und Bild in den Dichtungen Georg Trakls*, p. 180.

70. Jung, *The Practice of Psychotherapy*, p. 263.

Part II

1. The idea that death somehow results from love is an old one. *Eros* and *Thanatos* have frequently been linked in legend and literature. A more modern vindication of this feeling from a scientific point of view is the conclusion that death did not appear on the evolutionary chain until beings of two separate sexes developed, thus necessitating sexual reproduction. For the first billion years of evolution the simpler unisexual forms of life reproduced by dividing their cells. Only an accident of nature could result in the destruction of these organisms. When beings of two sexes evolved, two distinct types of cells went into the make-up of each individual; in addition to germ cells, of which the simpler life forms were entirely composed, there were now body cells. These body cells were responsible for the flesh and blood which served no procreative purpose beyond the transmitting of the germ cells from generation to generation and which could therefore be discarded by death; it began when sexual reproduction began. (The preceding information came from a lecture entitled "The Origin of Death," delivered at the University of Colorado on Aug. 6, 1969 by George Wald, Professor of Biology, Harvard University.)

2. The lovers and the unborn are ambiguous figures in "Allerseelen." It is not clear whether they are living or dead. They become central figures in Trakl's later poetry.

3. Novalis, *Schriften*, I: 364.

4. Hugo von Hofmannsthal, *Gesammelte Werke, Gedichte und Lyrische Dramen*, p. 280.

5. Rilke, *Sämtliche Werke*, ed. Zinn, I: 739–40.

6. Rilke, *Briefe aus Muzot*, pp. 332–33.

7. Ibid., p. 332.

8. See Goldmann, *Katabasis*, pp. 14–15; and Legrand, "La conception de la mort terrestre chez Trakl," *Cahiers du Sud*, pp. 32ff.

9. There are numerous allusions to the bitterness of death in Trakl's poetry (e.g., "Bitter ist der Tod, die Kost der Schuldbeladenen" [I: 150]). Klaus Simon distinguishes three types of death manifested in Trakl's poetry: the bitter, real death; the Orphic, aesthetic death; and the idyllic death. He begins by discussing the first type which he contrasts with death as it appears in Rilke's poetry. Simon maintains here that Trakl's poetry arises solely from the dualistic tension between life and death. Novalis, Hölderlin, and Rilke as Orphic poets have an aesthetic outlook on death which is foreign to Trakl. Simon then appears to contradict himself as he goes on to bring out the Orphic aspects of death in Trakl's poetry and does not revise his earlier statement separating Trakl decisively from the three Orphic poets. However, he does finally allow for the possibility of arriving at a "Grundbefindlichkeit" of Trakl regarding death which he later defines as a union of the Christian (real) and the Orphic (aesthetic) elements with an emphasis on the former. (See the chapters "Nacht und Tod" and "Orpheus" in Simon's *Traum und Orpheus*, pp. 92–154, esp. 107, 122, 152–53.) While recognizing fully the importance of the Christian and the Orphic elements in Trakl's treatment of death, I do not see a "Grundbefindlichkeit" in either of these categories or in their combination. I see in Trakl's death theme, whatever its manifestation, an atmosphere so pervasive that it defies such facile characterization by means of categories as ancient and ambiguous as the Christian and the Orphic. If categories are to be used at all, I prefer those of German Romanticism and Neoromanticism, which are in closer chronological proximity to Trakl and have also portrayed death as a pervasive reality and a state surpassing all others. In this sense, the portrayals of death in the works of these periods and in the works of Trakl are indeed similar, contrary to the opinion of Simon.

10. Meyknecht, *Das Bild des Menschen bei Georg Trakl.*

11. "An den Knaben Elis" was initially included as the first of three numbered parts in the second version of "Elis" (I: 373–75) but was later separated from it, thus becoming a distinct poem. The final version of "Elis" has only two parts. Trakl took the name Elis possibly from Elis Fröbom in Hugo von Hofmannsthal's drama *Das Bergwerk zu Falun*, the first act of which the author had published in his *Kleine Dramen* in 1906. The story of a miner killed in a cave-in and the sensational finding of his well-preserved corpse long afterward had been treated earlier by E. T. A. Hoffmann and Johann Peter Hebel.

12. Section 1 of the final version (I: 139–40) contains lines 46–64 of the second section of the *Brenner* version. Section 2 of the final version contains lines 66–72 of the third section of the *Brenner* version, plus some additional lines which cannot be directly traced to the latter. The third and last section of the final version contains lines 124–29 of the fifth section of the *Brenner* version and some additional lines which are also not derived from the latter.

13. Else Lasker-Schüler's poem entitled "Georg Trakl," written after her meeting with the poet and quoted in Szklenar, *Erinnerung an Georg Trakl* (p. 12), contains the following significant allusion to the subject matter of their conversation:

Wir stritten über Religion,
Aber immer wie zwei Spielgefährten,

Und bereiteten Gott von Mund zu Mund.
Im Anfang war das Wort.

Des Dichters Herz, eine feste Burg,
Seine Gedichte: Singende Thesen.

Er war wohl Martin Luther.

Lasker-Schüler's impressions of her meeting with Trakl, which occurred about three months after Trakl's conversation with Dallago recorded by Limbach, are further testimony to the religiosity, the "Christianity," of the poet. Such impressions of the poet's contemporaries should be considered against interpretations, such as those of Heidegger and Killy, which would deny or minimize this aspect of Trakl's poetry.

14. Goldmann, *Katabasis*, p. 47. But see also the negative aspects of crystal in Goldmann's view, pp. 47–48.

15. Elis' forehead bears the attribute of crystal in the second part of the final version of the poem "Elis" (I: 86). This is not to imply that crystal is used exclusively in association with childhood or that it always has a positive significance. The above interpretation illustrates only one of the several associative values of crystal.

16. Szklenar, *Erinnerung an Georg Trakl*, p. 186.

17. See Basil, *Georg Trakl in Selbstzeugnissen*, pp. 71–72.

18. See the chapter "Geburt in den Tod" in Goldmann, *Katabasis*, pp. 110–17.

19. Cf. the role of Tadzio in Thomas Mann's *Tod in Venedig*.

20. See note 13.

21. Heidegger, *Unterwegs zur Sprache*, p. 54. Falk criticizes Heidegger's statement as contrary to textual evidence but fails to take into account the line from "Der Wanderer" quoted above (*Leid und Verwandlung*, pp. 472–73).

22. Lachmann, "Trakl und Hölderlin, eine Deutung," p. 166. This is not to deny other points of contact between the two poets: e.g., the bread and wine motif mentioned above.

23. See Casey's discussion of "Enkel" in *Manshape That Shone*, pp. 91–92. "The 'Enkel' can generally be identified with the poet-protagonist" (p. 92).

24. Cf. the lines from the *Brenner* version of "Abendland": "Und balde / Endet des Menschen Wanderschaft,/ Gerechte Duldung" (I: 406). "Gesang des Abgeschiedenen" was written about the same time as this version of "Abendland": in March 1914 (see II: 262).

25. This also contradicts the finding of Falk who, in criticizing the conclusions of Heidegger, emphatically separates the two (*Leid und Verwandlung*, p. 473)

26. Cf. Jung, "Der Hermaphroditismus des Kindes" and "Das Kind als Anfangs- und Endwesen" in Jung and Kerényi, *Einführung in das Wesen der Mythologie*, pp. 137–44.

27. See Part I, note 32.

28. This motif also calls to mind the lines from Goethe's poem to Frau von Stein ("Warum gabst du uns die tiefen Blicke"): "Ach, du warst in abgelebten Zeiten/Meine Schwester oder meine Frau." Goethe seems to have espoused palingenesis, as did Lessing (see *Die Erziehung des Menschengeschlechts*, pars. 94–100), but not in the drastically pessimistic sense of Nietzsche.

29. Heidegger, *Unterwegs zur Sprache*, p. 57.

30. Ibid, p. 37.

31. Trakl is known to have asked for the help of his friend Buschbeck in obtaining the works of Eckhart, Tauler, and Seuse (see II: 756).

32. Pfeiffer, ed., *Deutsche Mystiker des vierzehnten Jahrhunderts*, II: 483–93. Eckhart's "Abgeschiedenheit" is related to the "dark night of the soul"—that period of almost unbearable misery and emptiness immediately preceding the mystic's final union with God. This concept is important in the works of Saint John of the Cross and later Catholic mysticism. One could analyze the works of Trakl, Kafka, and quite a few other modern writers as manifestations of an entire historical period enveloped in the dark night of the soul, a necessary penultimate state preparatory to ultimate fulfillment. Trakl, especially, would lend himself to this kind of interpretation, since images of fulfillment and redemption do shine forth in the midst of his otherwise disconsolate poetic oeuvre.

33. Heidegger, *Unterwegs zur Sprache*, p. 58.

34. Ibid., p. 70.

35. Heidegger's analysis of a line from Trakl's "Frühling der Seele" (I: 141) will serve as an example of his etymological approach. Heidegger's philosophy does not allow a distinction between a natural and supernatural form of existence. Since Plato, however, philosophers have frequently assigned the soul to the other, the supernatural realm. Thus the sentence "Es ist die Seele ein Fremdes auf Erden" appears to be perfectly in accord with Western thought since Plato. Heidegger denies this assumption. Deriving "fremd" from Old High German "fram," which means "forward," he considers Trakl's "Seele" as going forward toward the earth ("auf die Erde"). "Die Seele *sucht* die Erde erst, flieht sie nicht" (*Unterwegs zur Sprache*, p. 41). There is perceptive insight in this interpretation, since Trakl is, as a rule, not concerned with transcendence in his poetry. Heidegger's interpretation of this sentence, however, goes too far without actual textual justification. Moreover, it is not very likely that Trakl found time in his short life and short formal schooling to study Old High German.

36. Killy, *Über Georg Trakl*, p. 52.

37. Martin Heidegger was a subscriber to the *Brenner* from 1911 on (see Janik, "Carl Dallago and the Early Brenner," pp. 1–2).

38. Heidegger, *Sein und Zeit*, p. 83.

39. Ibid., p. 114.

40. Szklenar, *Erinnerung an Georg Trakl*, p. 122.

41. Heidegger, *Sein und Zeit*, p. 332.

42. Ibid., pp. 308–11.

43. See the chapter "Das Mögliche Ganzsein des Daseins und das Sein zum Tode," *Sein und Zeit*, pp. 314–54, esp. 340–48.

44. Ibid., pp. 431–38.

45. Ibid., pp. 333–34. The thrownness, "Geworfenheit," corresponds to the past, the possibility to the future, and the way we react in a given situation to the possibility into which we have been thrown (either by realizing it or ignoring it) to the present.

46. See King, *Heidegger's Philosophy*, p. 46.

47. Ibid., pp. 177–81. This possibility, death, is all the more negative, since it is really the impossibility of existence.

48. See, for example, "Brief über den 'Humanismus'": "Mit dem Heilen zumal erscheint in der Lichtung des Seins das Böse. . . . Beide, das Heile und das Grimmige, können jedoch im Sein nur wesen, insofern das Sein selber das Strittige ist." "Das Nichtende im Sein ist das Wesen dessen, was ich das Nichts nenne. Darum, weil es

das Sein denkt, denkt das Denken das Nichts. Sein erst gewährt dem Heilen Aufgang in Huld und Andrang zu Unheil dem Grimm" (Heidegger, *Wegmarken*, pp. 359–60).

Another quote from note 14 at the end of "Die Zeit des Weltbildes" further describes the nature of "das Nichts" and brings it into relationship with the question of subject versus object: "Von der Metaphysik her begriffen . . . enthüllt sich zunächst das verborgene Wesen des Seins, die Verweigerung, als das schlechthin Nicht-Seiende, als das Nichts. Aber das Nichts ist als das Nichthafte des Seienden der schärfste Widerpart des bloss Nichtigen. Das Nichts ist niemals nichts, es ist ebensowenig ein Etwas im Sinne eines Gegenstandes; es ist das Sein selbst, dessen Wahrheit der Mensch dann übereignet wird, wenn er sich als Subjekt überwunden hat, und d.h., wenn er das Seiende nicht mehr als Objekt vorstellt" (Heidegger, *Holzwege*, pp. 112–13).

49. Rey, "Heidegger-Trakl." Rey, in one instance, goes as far as to distort Heidegger by not quoting him fully. He claims that Heidegger refers to Lucifer simply as the light bearer. ("Denn er sieht in Luzifer einfach den 'Lichtträger' " [p. 115]. See Trakl's poem "An Luzifer" [I: 333–35].) Heidegger writes, however, " 'An Luzifer,' d.h. an den Lichtträger, der den Schatten des Bösen wirft" (*Unterwegs zur Sprache*, p. 61).

50. Ibid., p. 59.

51. Ibid., p. 60 (italics Heidegger's).

52. Heidegger, *Holzwege*, p. 271.

53. Heidegger, *Unterwegs zur Sprache*, p. 67.

54. A comparison with Goethe suggests itself again at this point. The primacy of the future is totally antithetical to Goethe's realistic view of time. For him the present is the all-important time. The present is formed from elements of the past and gives, in turn, elements to the formation of the future. It is therefore of utmost importance to work actively in the present in order to insure a good future (see Viëtor, *Goethe*, p. 472). In a life properly lived the present moment can gather the past and the future into itself and even attain symbolic value as a representative of eternity: "Dann ist Vergangenheit beständig,/ Das Künftige voraus lebendig,/ Der Augenblick ist Ewigkeit" ("Vermächtnis").

55. Szklenar, *Erinnerung an Georg Trakl*, pp. 10–11.

56. Ibid., p. 11.

57. Hofmannsthal, *Gesammelte Werke*, p. 280.

Part III

1. Szklenar, *Erinnerung an Georg Trakl*, p. 125.

2. It is also possible that the young novice of "Psalm" (I: 55) and the beginning of the second section of "Helian" (I:70) is a figure prompted by the novice Alyosha Karamazov.

3. See Part I, note 32.

4. Nietzsche, *Werke*, III: 1350.

5. The hunter appears elsewhere in Trakl's poetry as the instrument of evil: e.g., in the last line of the prologue to *Don Juans Tod* the hero is called "Ein Jäger, der die Pfeile schickt nach Gott" (I: 447).

6. See Part I, note 17.

7. See Spoerri, *Georg Trakl*; Heselhaus, "Die Elis-Gedichte von Georg Trakl"; Lindenberger, "The Play of Opposites in Georg Trakl's Poetry."

8. Grimm, "Die Sonne: Bemerkungen zu einem Motiv Georg Trakls," p. 242.

9. Notably Spoerri and Lindenberger. (See note 7.)

10. "Die Bilder bleiben bestehen, aber das Spiel mit ihnen geschieht nicht mehr im Hinblick auf die Wirklichkeit" (Killy, *Wandlungen des lyrischen Bildes*, p. 134).

11. Heselhaus, "Das metaphorische Gedicht von Georg Trakl."

12. Schier, "Von den Metaphern zur figuralen Sprache."

13. *Goethes Werke*, Hamburger Ausgabe, XII: 470. Hereafter, all references to this edition will be by means of "H.A." followed by volume and page numbers.

14. This quotation is from Goethe's *Italienische Reise*. A similar quotation from the same work reads: "Diese hohen Kunstwerke sind zugleich als die höchsten Naturwerke von Menschen nach wahren und natürlichen Gesetzen hervorgebracht worden. Alles Willkürliche, Eingebildete fällt zusammen, da ist Notwendigkeit, da ist Gott" (H.A., XI: 395).

15. From "Die Natur" (fragment from "Tiefurter Journal" 1783). Although it is known that Goethe was not the author of this essay, Goethe himself maintained later in his life that it agreed with his thought on the subject at that time (H.A., XIII: 48).

16. According to Heisenberg's "uncertainty principle," it is impossible to specify simultaneously with accuracy both the position and velocity of an atomic particle (electron), since it has both corpuscular and wavelike characteristics (see *Brockhaus Enzyklopädie*, 1974, s.v. "Unschärfebeziehung").

17. This word is from the poem which begins: "Es winkt zu Fühlung fast aus allen Dingen" (Rilke, *Sämtliche Werke* [Wiesbaden: Insel], II: 92–93).

18. Ibid., I: 714.

19. Some other lines from the Eighth Elegy shed further light on the circle-of-death pattern discussed in Part II—the blending of past, present, and future (death) of the human being into a time-whole. Rilke seems to posit the same pattern for his animal when he writes: "das freie Tier / hat seinen Untergang stets hinter sich / und vor sich Gott" (ibid., I: 714). Later in the same elegy he writes: "Und wo wir Zukunft sehn, dort sieht es Alles / und sich in Allem und geheilt für immer" (ibid., I: 715).

20. Ibid., I: 714.

21. Karl Ludwig Schneider has coined the term "dynamisierende Metapher" to refer to such images. See *Der bildhafte Ausdruck in den Dichtungen Georg Heyms, Georg Trakls und Ernst Stadlers*, pp. 143–46. He also speaks of an "Umriszschwäche" of Trakl's human figures (p. 97) which corresponds to my characterization: "the blurring of contours." His conclusion, however, that these devices serve to underline the linguistic independence and determination of an "expressionistisches Ich" (p. 179) is contrary to the findings of the present analysis (see pp. 103–105).

22. Pinthus, *Menschheitsdämmerung*, p. 47.

23. Strohschneider-Kohrs, "Die Entwicklung der lyrischen Sprache in der Dichtung Georg Trakls," p. 222.

24. Ibid., pp. 225–26.

25. Noteworthy in this connection is also the frequent use of the word "Schatten": e.g., "Ein Schatten bin ich ferne finsteren Dörfern" (I: 46).

26. Spoerri, *Georg Trakl*, p. 106.

27. Böhme, *Sämtliche Schriften*: "Und verstehen [wir] weiter, dass Gott selber das Sehen und Empfinden des Nichts sey, und wird darum ein Nichts genant, (ob es gleich Gott selber ist) dass es unbegreiflich und unaussprechlich ist" (IX: 5). "Gott ist Nichts, gegen der Creatur zu rechnen, und ist der Ungrund und Alles" (IX: 110).

28. To these could be added the more or less indefinite pronouns "jener" and "jemand."

29. Killy also considers the term "metaphor" inadequate when applied to Trakl's poetry. Killy writes in *Über Georg Trakl*: "Wenn der Beginn von 'Nachtseele' lautet:

Schweigsam stieg von schwarzen Wäldern ein blaues Wild
Die Seele nieder,
Da es Nacht war, über moosige Stufen ein schneeiger Quell.

so hat dieser Satz ein Prädikat, jedoch drei parallele Subjekte: 'Seele'—'blaues Wild'—'schneeiger Quell.' Mit dem Begriff der Metapher ist angesichts solchen ständigen Übergangs nichts getan; das 'wie' des Vergleichs setzt die Bestimmtheit der Erscheinungen voraus. Hier ist jedes das andere . . ." (p. 49).

30. See Goldmann, *Katabasis:* "Golden ist also die Farbe geheiligter, anfänglicher Lebenskraft, göttlichen Seins, des glücklichen Einklangs. Sie ist positiv, aktiv" (p. 41). "Schwarz ist bei Trakl die Farbe der Zerstörung, der Verwesung, des Todes und zugleich des Tötens" (p. 35).

31. See Kritsch,"The Synesthetic Metaphors in the Poetry of Georg Trakl." The author divides these metaphors into two main groups: "photisms," whose secondary sensation is optical and "phonisms," whose secondary sensation is acoustic. Her conclusion that Trakl uses such metaphors to give greater weight to his subjective world is questionable. It is precisely this subjective element which the poet strives consciously to suppress in his later works (see pp. 103–105).

32. Novalis, *Schriften*, I: 82–83.

33. Neumann *Der schöpferische Mensch*, p. 87.

34. Ibid., p. 97.

35. Benn, *Essays, Reden, Vorträge*, p. 21.

36. Ibid., p. 22.

37. Ibid., pp. 15–16.

38. Benn, *Autobiographische und vermischte Schriften*, p. 8.

39. Benn mentions Trakl's name twice in his essay "Expressionismus," ibid., p. 242.

40. Ibid., p. 243.

41. See Jung, *Mysterium Coniunctionis*, pp. 462, 533–43.

42. Ibid., p. 535.

43. Ibid., p. 538.

44. Béguin, *Gérard de Nerval suivi de Poésie et mystique*. For the influence of Rimbaud on Trakl's poetry, see Grimm, "Georg Trakls Verhältnis zu Rimbaud"; Böschenstein, "Wirkungen des französischen Symbolismus auf die deutsche Lyrik der Jahrhundertwende"; and Lindenberger *Georg Trakl*.

45. Béguin, *Gérard de Nerval*, p. 106.

46. Ibid., p. 107.

47. Ibid., pp. 108–9.

48. Béguin distinguishes between modern poetry and mysticism, however, by pointing out that while the mystic experiences a sense of well-being and salvation in God, modern poetry often expresses a sense of hopelessness and even evil through rebellion against God (ibid., pp. 115–116). Béguin does not, however, include in his consideration the mystical "dark night of the soul," a state resembling the hopelessness in much of modern poetry.

49. Killy, *Über Georg Trakl*, pp. 36–37.

50. Killy, *Wandlungen des lyrischen Bildes*, p. 134.

51. Killy, *Über Georg Trakl*, p. 14.

52. Ibid., p. 13.

53. Ibid., pp. 46–47.

54. Killy, "Bestand und Bewegung in Gedichten Georg Trakls," see esp. pp. 249–52.

55. See Böschenstein, "Wirkungen," p. 394.

56. Fromm, *Beyond the Chains of Illusion*, pp. 169–72.

57. Teilhard de Chardin, *Le phénomène humain*.

58. Guardini, *The End of the Modern World*, pp. 76ff.

59. Ibid., p. 110.

60. Ibid., pp. 111–12.

61. Guardini believes that the conformity of the new age, the loss of individuality, also has a positive side. Men are standing together in their endeavors as they have never done before. Even if all other human values decline, a sense of comradeship will remain to compensate for the loss of the others, perhaps even to regenerate them (ibid., pp. 84–85).

62. The words "Des verboten Liebenden" (II: 434), a variant in a preliminary version of "Die Heimkehr," are in keeping with Trakl's incest theme. They occur in approximately the place now occupied by the line "Liebe, Hoffnung."

Selected Bibliography

Trakl's Works

Trakl, Georg. *Dichtungen und Briefe*. Ed. Walther Killy and Hans Szklenar. 2 vols. Salzburg: Otto Müller, 1969.

On Trakl

Alt, Wilhelm, "Georg Trakl." *Wort in der Zeit. Österreichische Literaturzeitschrift* 3, No. 2 (1957): 1–5.

B▮▮▮▮▮▮ ▮▮▮▮. *Georg Trakl in Selbstzeugnissen und Bilddokumenten*. Rowohlts Mono-▮▮▮▮▮▮. Hamburg: Rowohlt, 1965.

Blass, Regine. *Die Dichtung Georg Trakls. Von der Trivialsprache zum Kunstwerk*. Philologische Studien und Quellen, Heft 43. Berlin: Erich Schmidt, 1968.

Bleisch, Ernst. *Georg Trakl*. Mühlacker: Stieglitz, 1964.

Bolli, Erich. *Georg Trakls "Dunkler Wohllaut." Ein Beitrag zum Verständnis seines dichterischen Sprechens*. Zürcher Beiträge, Bd. 48. Zürich: Artemis, 1978.

Böschenstein, Bernhard. "Wirkungen des französischen Symbolismus auf die deutsche Lyrik der Jahrhundertwende." *Euphorion* 58 (1964): 375–95.

Casey, T. J. *Manshape That Stone: An Interpretation of Trakl*. Oxford: Basil Blackwell, 1964.

Colleville, Maurice. "Du nouveau sur Trakl." *Etudes Germaniques* 11 (1956): 224–46.

Dietz, Ludwig. *Die lyrische Form Georg Trakls*. Trakl-Studien V. Salzburg: Otto Müller, 1959.

Doppler, Alfred. "Georg Trakl und Otto Weininger." In *Peripherie und Zentrum. Studien zur österreichischen Literatur*, pp. 43–54. Salzburg: "Das Bergland-Buch," 1971.

———. "Die Stufe der Präexistenz in den Dichtungen Georg Trakls." *Zeitschrift für deutsche Philologie* 87 (1968): 273–84.

Eykman, Christoph. *Die Funktion des Hässlichen in der Lyrik Georg Heyms, Georg Trakls, und Gottfried Benns*. Bonner Arbeiten zur deutschen Literatur, Bd. 11. Bonn: Bouvier, 1965.

Falk, Walter. "Heidegger und Trakl." *Literaturwissenschaftliches Jahrbuch der Görresgesellschaft* 4 (1963): 191–204.

———. *Leid und Verwandlung, Rilke, Kafka, Trakl und der Epochenstil des Impres-*

sionismus und Expressionismus. Trakl-Studien VI. Salzburg: Otto Müller, 1961.

Ficker, Ludwig von. "Erinnerungen an Georg Trakl." *Etudes Germaniques* 15 (1960): 113–19.

Focke, Alfred, S. J. *Georg Trakl. Leibe und Tod.* München und Wien: Herold, 1955.

Goldmann, Heinrich. *Katabasis. Eine tiefenpsychologische Studie zur Symbolik der Dichtungen Georg Trakls.* Trakl-Studien IV. Salzburg: Otto Müller, 1957.

Grimm, Reinhold. "Georg Trakls Verhältnis zu Rimbaud." *Germanisch-romanische Monatsschrift,* 2d ser., 9 (1959): 288–315.

————. "Die Sonne. Bemerkungen zu einem Motiv Georg Trakls." *Deutsche Vierteljahresschrift* 35 (1961): 224–46.

————. "Zur Wirkungsgeschichte Maurice Maeterlincks in der deutschsprachigen Literatur." *Revue de Littérature Comparée* 33 (1959): 535–44.

Gröbenschütz, Edith. "Zur Datierung im Werk Georg Trakls. Im Zusammenhang mit einem kürzlich bekanntgewordenen Brief." *Euphorion* 58 (1964): 411–27.

Haeckel, H. "Verfall und Verfallenheit. Anlässlich eines Deutungsversuches an einem Gedicht Georg Trakls." *Zeitschrift für deutsche Philologie* 78 (1959): 369–94.

Hamburger, Michael. "Georg Trakl." In *Reason and Energy,* pp. 239–71. London: Routledge and Kegan Paul, 1957.

Hellmich, Albert. *Klang und Erlösung. Das Problem musikalischer Struktur in der Lyrik Georg Trakls.* Trakl-Studien VIII. Salzburg: Otto Müller, 1971.

Hermand, Jost. "Der Knabe Elis. Zum Problem der Existenzstufen bei Georg Trakl." *Monatshefte* 51 (1959): 225–36.

Heselhaus, Clemens. "Die Elis-Gedichte von Georg Trakl." *Deutsche Vierteljahresschrift* 28 (1954): 384–413.

————. "Das metaphorische Gedicht von Georg Trakl." In *Deutsche Lyrik der Moderne von Nietzsche bis Ivan Goll. Die Rückkehr zur Bildlichkeit der* ⸺⸺⸺, ⸺⸺⸺. 228–57. Düsseldorf: A. Bagel, 1961.

————, and Walter Höllerer. "Georg Trakl." In *Die deutsche Lyrik, Form und Geschichte,* edited by Benno von Wiese, II: 401–24. Düsseldorf: A. Bagel, 1956.

Kars, Gustav. "Georg Trakl in wechselnder Deutung." *Literatur und Kritik* 93 (1975): 132–44.

Kemper, Hans-Georg. *Georg Trakls Entwürfe. Aspekte zu ihrem Verständnis.* Studien zur deutschen Literatur, Bd. 19. Tübingen: Niemeyer, 1970.

————. "Trakl-Forschung der sechziger Jahre. Korrekturen über Korrekturen." *Deutsche Vierteljahresschrift* 45, Sonderheft (1971): 496–571.

Killy, Walther. "Bestand und Bewegung in Gedichten Georg Trakls." In *Festschrift für Bernhard Blume. Aufsätze zur deutschen und europäischen Literatur,* edited by Egon Schwarz, Hunter Hannum, and Edgar Lohner, pp. 246–57. Göttingen: Vandenhoeck and Ruprecht, 1967.

————. "Gedichte im Gedicht. Beschäftigung mit Trakl-Handschriften." *Merkur* 12 (1958): 1108–21.

————. "Nochmals über Trakls 'Passion.' Mit Rücksicht auf die handschriftliche Überlieferung." *Euphorion* 52 (1958): 400–413.

————. *Über Georg Trakl.* Göttingen: Vandenhoeck and Ruprecht, 1960.

————. *Wandlungen des lyrischen Bildes.* 4th ed. Göttingen: Vandenhoeck and Ruprecht, 1964.

Kritsch, Erna. "The Synesthetic Metaphors in the Poetry of Georg Trakl." *Monatshefte* 54 (1962): 69–77.

Lachmann, Eduard. "Georg Trakls herbstliche 'Passion.' *Euphorion* 52 (1958): 397–399.

———. "Gespräch über ein Trakl-Gedicht. Zum Gedächtnis des 70. Geburtstages Georg Trakls am 3. Feb. 1957." *Wirkendes Wort* 7 (1957): 159–162.

———. *Kreuz und Abend. Eine Interpretation der Dichtungen Georg Trakls.* Trakl-Studien I. Salzburg: Otto Müller, 1954.

———. "Trakl und Hölderlin. Eine Deutung." In *Georg Trakl, Nachlass und Biographie,* vol. III of *Gesammelte Werke,* edited by Wolfgang Schneditz, pp. 163–212. Salzburg: Otto Müller, 1949.

Legrand, Jacques. "La conception de la mort terrestre chez Trakl." *Cahiers du Sud* 45 (1957): 21–38.

Lindenberger, Herbert. "The Early Poems of Georg Trakl." *Germanic Review* 32 (1957): 45–61.

———. "Georg Trakls 'Traum und Umnachtung.'" In *Festschrift für Bernhard Blume, Aufsätze zur deutschen und europäischen Literatur,* edited by Egon Schwarz, Hunter Hannum, and Edgar Lohner, pp. 258–70. Göttingen: Vandenhoeck and Ruprecht, 1967.

———. *Georg Trakl.* Twayne's World Authors Series 171. New York: Twayne, 1971.

———. "The Play of Opposites in Georg Trakl's Poetry." *German Life and Letters* 11 (1958): 193–204.

Lüders, Detlev. "'Abendmuse,' 'Untergang,' 'Anif.' Drei Gedichte von Georg Trakl." *Wirkendes Wort* 11 (1961): 89–102.

Magnuson, Karl. "Consonant Repetition in the Lyric of Georg Trakl." *Germanic Review* 37 (1962): 263–81.

Methlagl, Walter. "Georg Trakl: 'Schwesters Garten.' Interpretation aus dem Gesamtwerk." In *Gemanistische Studien,* edited by Johannes Erben and Eugen Thurnher. Innsbrucker Beiträge zur Kulturwissenschaft, Bd. 15. Innsbruck, 1969.

Meyknecht, Werner. *Das Bild des Menschen bei Georg Trakl.* Quakenbruck: Kleinert, 1935.

Muschg, Walter. *Von Trakl zu Brecht. Dichter des Expressionismus.* München: Piper, 1961.

Palmier, Jean-Michel. *Situation de Georg Trakl.* Paris: Belfond, 1972.

Philipp, Eckhard. *Die Funktion des Wortes in den Gedichten Georg Trakls. Linguistische Aspekte ihrer Interpretation.* Studien zur deutschen Literatur, Bd. 26. Tübingen: Niemeyer, 1971.

Piontek, Heinz. "Georg Trakl." In *Triffst du nur das Zauberwort. Stimmen von heute zur deutschen Lyrik,* edited by Jürgen Petersen, pp. 244–54. Berlin: Propyläen, 1961.

Preisendanz, Wolfgang. "Auflösung und Verdinglichung in den Gedichten Georg Trakls." In *Immanente Ästhetik/Ästhetische Reflexion: Lyrik als Paradigma der Moderne,* edited by Wolfgang Iser, pp. 227–61. München: Fink, 1966.

Rey, W. H. "Heidegger—Trakl. Einstimmiges Zwiegespräch." *Deutsche Vierteljahresschrift* 30 (1956): 89–136.

Ritzer, Walter. *Trakl-Bibliographie.* Trakl-Studien III. Salzburg: Otto Müller, 1956.

Rovini, Robert. "Georg Trakl. Variations sur le mouvant." *Cahiers du Sud* 45 (1957): 3–20.

Saas, Christa. *Georg Trakl.* Sammlung Metzler, Bd. 124. Stuttgart: Metzler, 1974.

Scherer, Michael. "Georg Trakl. 'Zu Abend mein Herz.'" In *Interpretationen moderner Lyrik,* edited by Fachgruppe Deutsch-Geschichte im Bayerischen Philologenverband, pp. 60–63. 5th ed. Wiesbaden: Moritz Diesterweg, 1958.

Schier, Rudolf D. "Von den Metaphern zur figuralen Sprache. Abgrenzung der Begriffe. Dargestellt an Georg Trakls 'Gesang des Abgeschiedenen.'" *Der Deutschunterricht* 20 (1968): 49–68.

Schlenstedt, Silvia. "Georg Trakl." *Weimarer Beiträge* 5 (1959): 513–26.

Schneditz, Wolfgang. "Versuch einer Deutung des Menschen und des Dichters." In *Georg Trakl, Nachlass und Biographie*, vol. III of *Gesammelte Werke*, edited by Wolfgang Schneditz, pp. 66–126. Salzburg: Otto Müller, 1949.

Schneider, Karl Ludwig. *Der bildhafte Ausdruck in den Dichtungen Georg Heyms, Georg Trakls und Ernst Stadlers. Studien zum lyrischen Sprachstil des deutschen Expressionismus.* 3d ed. Heidelberg: Carl Winter, 1968.

Sharp, Francis Michael. *The Poet's Madness: A Reading of Georg Trakl.* Ithaca and London: Cornell University Press, 1981.

Simon, Klaus. *Traum und Orpheus. Eine Studie zu Georg Trakls Dichtungen.* Trakl-Studien II. Salzburg: Otto Müller, 1955.

Spoerri, Theodor. *Georg Trakl, Strukturen in Persönlichkeit und Werk. Eine psychiatrisch-anthropographische Untersuchung.* Bern: Francke, 1954.

Staiger, Emil. "Zu einem Gedicht Georg Trakls." *Euphorion* 55 (1961): 279–96.

Stinchcombe, J. "Trakl's 'Elis' Poems and E. T. A. Hoffmann's 'Die Bergwerke zu Falun.'" *Modern Language Review* 59 (1964): 609–15.

Strohschneider-Kohrs, Ingrid. "Die Entwicklung der lyrischen Sprache in der Dichtung Georg Trakls." *Literaturwissenschaftliches Jahrbuch der Görresgesellschaft* 1 (1960): 211–26.

Szklenar, Hans. "Ein vorläufiger Bericht über den Nachlass Georg Trakls." *Euphorion* 54 (1961): 295–311.

———, ed. *Erinnerung an Georg Trakl. Zeugnisse und Briefe.* 3d ed. Darmstadt: Wissenschaftliche Buchgesellschaft, 1966.

Thiele, Herbert. "Das Bild des Menschen in den Kaspar-Hauser-Gedichten von Paul Verlaine und Georg Trakl." *Wirkendes Wort* 14 (1964): 351–56.

Weber, Albrecht. "Georg Trakl." In *Wege zum Gedicht*, edited by Ruprecht Hirschenauer and Albrecht Weber, pp. 339–48. München: Schnell and Steiner, 1956.

Wetzel, Heinz. *Klang und Bild in den Dichtungen Georg Trakls.* Palaestra Bd. 248. Göttingen: Vandenhoeck and Ruprecht, 1968.

———. *Konkordanz zu den Dichtungen Georg Trakls.* Trakl-Studien, Bd. VII. Salzburg: Otto Müller, 1971.

———. "Zum Verständnis der Dichtungen Trakls." *Monatshefte* 58 (1966): 97–114.

Wölfel, Kurt. "Entwicklungsstufen im lyrischen Werk Trakls." *Euphorion* 52 (1958): 50–81.

General Background

Béguin, Albert. *Gérard de Nerval suivi de Poésie et mystique.* Paris: Delamain and Boutelleau, 1936.

Benn, Gottfried. *Autobiographische und vermischte Schriften*, vol. IV of *Gesammelte Werke in vier Bänden*, edited by Dieter Wellershoff. Wiesbaden: Limes, 1961.

———. *Essays, Reden, Vorträge*, vol. I of *Gesammelte Werke in vier Bänden*, edited by Dieter Wellershoff. 2d ed. Wiesbaden: Limes, 1962.

Böhme, Jakob. *Sämtliche Schriften.* Edited by Will-Erich Peuckert. Stuttgart: Fr. Frommanns, 1955ff.

Casper, M. Kent. "Primitivism and the Creative Process in the Works of Gottfried Benn." Ph.D. dissertation, Harvard Univ., April 1968.

Delcourt, Marie. *Hermaphrodite: Myths and Rites of the Bisexual Figure in Classical Antiquity.* Translated by Jennifer Nicholson. London: Longacre Press, 1961.

Fromm, Erich. *Beyond the Chains of Illusion: My Encounter with Marx and Freud.* The Credo Series. New York: Trident Press, 1962.

Goethe, Johann Wolfgang von. *Goethes Werke.* Hamburger Ausgabe. Hamburg: Christian Wegner, 1948 ff.

Guardini, Romano. *The End of the Modern World: A Search for Orientation.* Translated by Joseph Theman and Herbert Burke. London: Sheed and Ward, 1957.

Heidegger, Martin. *Holzwege,* Abt. I, Bd. V of *Gesamtausgabe.* Frankfurt am Main: Vittorio Klostermann, 1977.

———. *Sein und Zeit,* Abt. I, Bd. II of *Gesamtausgabe.* Frankfurt am Main: Vittorio Klostermann, 1977.

———. *Unterwegs zur Sprache.* Pfullingen: Neske, 1959.

———. *Wegmarken,* Abt. I, Bd. IX of *Gesamtausgabe.* Frankfurt am Main: Vittorio Klostermann, 1976.

Hofmannsthal, Hugo von. *Gesammelte Werke, Gedichte und lyrische Dramen.* Stockholm: Bermann-Fischer Verlag, 1946.

Janik, Allan. "Carl Dallago and the Early Brenner." *Modern Austrian Literature* 11, no. 2 (1978): 1–17.

Jung, C. G. *Mysterium Coniunctionis: An Inquiry into the Separation and Synthesis of Psychic Opposites in Alchemy,* vol. XIV of *The Collected Works,* edited by Herbert Read, Michael Fordham, and Gerhard Adler; translated by R. F. C. Hull. Bollingen Series XX. New York: Pantheon, 1963.

———. *The Practice of Psychotherapy: Essays on the Psychology of Transference and Other Subjects,* vol. XVI of *The Collected Works,* edited by Herbert Read, Michael Fordham, and Gerhard Adler; translated by R. F. C. Hull. Bollingen Series XX. 2d ed. New York: Pantheon, 1966.

———. *Psychology and Alchemy,* vol. XII of *The Collected Works,* edited by Herbert Read, Michael Fordham, Gerhard Adler, and William McGuire; translated by R. F. C. Hull. Bollingen Series XX. 2d ed. New York: Pantheon, 1968.

———. *The Structure and Dynamics of the Psyche,* vol. VIII of *The Collected Works,* edited by Herbert Read, Michael Fordham, and Gerhard Adler; translated by R. F. C. Hull. Bollingen Series XX. New York: Pantheon, 1960.

———, and Karl Kerényi. *Einführung in das Wesen der Mythologie. Das göttliche Kind, das göttliche Mädchen.* 4th ed. Zürich: Rhein, 1951.

King, Magda. *Heidegger's Philosophy: A Guide to His Basic Thought.* New York: Macmillan, 1964.

Mörike, Eduard. *Werke.* Edited by Harry Maync. Leipzig: Bibliographisches Institut, 1914.

Neumann, Erich. *Der schöpferische Mensch.* Zürich: Rhein, 1959.

Nietzsche, Friedrich. *Werke.* Edited by Karl Schlechta. München: Carl Hanser, 1956 ff.

Novalis. *Schriften.* Edited by Paul Kluckhohn and Richard Samuel. Darmstadt: Wissenschaftliche Buchgesellschaft, 1977.

Pfeiffer, Franz, ed. *Deutsche Mystiker des vierzehnten Jahrhunderts.* Aalen: Scientia, 1962.

Pinthus, Kurt, ed. *Menschheitsdämmerung. Ein Dokument des Expressionismus.* Rowohlts Klassiker, Deutsche Literatur, Bd. 4. Hamburg: Rowohlt, 1959.

Rank, Otto. *Das Inzest-Motiv in Dichtung und Sage. Grundzüge einer Psychologie des dichterischen Schaffens.* Leipzig: Franz Deuticke, 1912.

Reinach, Salomon. *Cultes, mythes, et religions.* 2d ed. 4 vols. Paris: Leroux, 1908.

Reitzenstein, Richard, and Hans Heinrich Schraeder. *Studien zum antiken Synkretismus aus Iran und Griechenland.* Darmstadt: Wissenschaftliche Buchgesellschaft, 1965.

Rilke, Rainer Maria. *Briefe aus Muzot, 1921 bis 1926.* Edited by Ruth Sieber-Rilke and Carl Sieber. Leipzig: Insel, 1935.

———. *"Sämtliche Werke.* Edited by Ernst Zinn. Frankfurt am Main: Insel, 1955ff.

Röck, Karl. *Tagebuch 1891–1946.* Edited by Christine Kofler. Salzburg: Otto Müller, 1976.

Rolland de Renéville, A. "Poetes et mystiques." *Mesures,* no. 2 (April 1936): 107–133.

Schlegel, Friedrich. *Dichtungen. Kritische Friedrich-Schlegel-Ausgabe.* Edited by Hans Eichner. München: Schöningh, 1962.

Teilhard de Chardin, Pierre. *Le phénomène humain,* vol. I of *Oeuvres.* Paris: Éditions du Seuil, 1955.

Viëtor, Karl. *Goethe.* Bern: Francke, 1949.

Weininger, Otto. *Geschlecht und Charakter. Eine prinzipielle Untersuchung.* Wien: Wilhelm Braumüller, 1909.

Index